The Cottontown Killer

James Watts is an amateur historian and student of science who has made a home in his adopted county of Lancashire

Thomas Watts works in broadcasting in Lancashire and London

James Watts and Thomas Watts

The Cottontown Killer

Table of Contents

Beginnings

In the very early hours of 15th May, 1948, as the waxing moon sent a sullen light through the drizzle, one of Britain's greatest detectives was rudely awoken by a telephone call from Scotland Yard. This call precipitated one of the largest, and most extraordinary, manhunts in the annals of policing in an attempt to solve one of the ghastliest murders in British history. The murder is now largely forgotten except in the memories a small number of elderly residents of a weary northern industrial town, dwindling in numbers as the years pass. Yet, the legacy of the investigation, and how it affected future crime investigation, is such that it merits recording in greater detail, because in May 1948, a devil walked through the town of Blackburn, and his touch brought terror to a nation

James Watts & Thomas Watts

Chapter 1

Cottontown

Blackburn: 50BC – 1948 AD
'Arte et Labore: By Craft and Hard Work'
the motto on Blackburn's coat of arms

To understand this terrible crime, we need to understand all the key players, and the character of Blackburn town itself is as important as that of the humans that were intimately involved.

As northerners say, in 1948 Blackburn was dying on its arse. It had at times been tormented by fluctuant fortunes, having been both prosperous, and poverty stricken; and had been both the centre of momentous events, and bypassed by history. It was a complex and wounded environment, at once both mythic and dreamy, and practical and pragmatic.

Of the pre-history of Blackburn, little is known. The windswept, heathered landscape was home to a few gnarled sheep and hardy cattle, patrolled by warlike Celtic tribes such as the Brigantes, who left no formal records. Blackburn's recorded history begins of course with the Romans. Settling at nearby Ribchester, their only acknowledgement of the area is a broken monument to a once sacred spring, a plaque to which remains at Railway Street in the modern town. For the Romans, Britain was the land of mists at the edge of the world, where the Ninth Legion was magicked away without trace. When they left Britain, a Dark Age fell across the land and nothing of any significance is known until Christianity seeped across the country, inspiring the construction of the great wooden church of the Parish of *Blagbourne* on the site of what is nowadays Blackburn Cathedral. Saxons and Vikings waged war across the country, and were in turn conquered by the Normans, who tore across the North in what entered legend as *the Harrowing*. They established a market at Blackburn, based on the trade of the bleached cloth which is thought to give the town its name, but planted a castle at Clitheroe, which became the administrative centre of the county.

Blackburn then remained on the periphery of great events for hundreds of years. The Wars of the Roses ended with the estranged King Henry VI being captured at nearby Waddington, having been betrayed by the monks at Whalley Abbey, now a ruin. In the meantime, the commercial heart of the county was seized by local nobles. The de Hoghtons were a local family, who came to prominence by taxing the trade route from Preston, building a fortress home known as Hoghton Towers near Chorley. It is local legend that a young man named William Shakespeare taught the de

Hoghton children there before finding fame and fortune in London, and that King James I and VI rode into the great hall mounted on his white horse as he travelled south to claim the throne from the bony hands of the Virgin Queen. It is there that he supposedly knighted a side of beef as *Sir Loin*. Famously afraid of witchcraft, it was in James' reign that one of the most notorious witches' covens was apparently uncovered in the heart of Lancashire.

In the forests and mist covered moors to the north of Blackburn is Pendle Hill. As the name derives from both the ancient Anglo-Saxon and Viking words for hill, this landmark effectively glories in the prosaic translated name of '*hill hill hill*'. The mount overlooked scattered farms, villages and isolated hamlets where jealousy, muddled with fear and superstition, fostered rumours of crippling curses and black masses, and familiars stalking the night waiting to trap the unwary and ungodly. Such was the hysteria that in 1612 seven men and women were dragged from Pendle for trial, accused of consorting with the Devil at nearby Malkin Tower. They were all committed in chains at Lancaster Castle, the charges against them including cannibalism. In an ironic and coincidental testament to this episode of incipient devil worship, the main road from Manchester, through Darwen and Blackburn to Whalley, is now designated as the A666.

The town continued to grow and develop, the Civil War causing little disruption other than the ineffectual bombardment of the centre by local cavalier Sir Gilbert de Hoghton, who duly retired back home afterwards for the rest of the conflict, honour having presumably been satisfied. Later, Bonnie Prince Charley's Jacobites ravaged

Preston on their advance south, and then their surly retreat, leaving Blackburn alone.

During these terrible times, Blackburn and its surrounds continued to foster a reputation for textile manufacture, based on isolated cottage industries. This evolved into a more organised form of weaving, at homes on looms. Blackburn's position on several major highways, and its access to the river, essential in the cloth making process, made it an ideal locale for the growth of the industry. Cotton, imported from British Dominions abroad arrived by sea and barge up the new canals that were bored into the countryside, to be woven into high quality merchandise, which was then sold back to the countries it originated from. By the end of the 18th Century there were thousands of looms in the borough, and a few industrious yeomen began to organise peasants into working groups. These were the forerunners of what would become the new mercantile middle class and would eventually rise to great wealth. The Fieldens, the Hornbys, the Holdens and the Sudells would all bloom from modest Lancastrian backgrounds to become titans of industry. They gathered the weavers into mass producing co-operatives, and then housed them in enormous and dehumanising dark, satanic mills that pitted the landscape. Science advanced the process of manufacture very quickly, and new machines, coupled with the overwhelming economic power of the mills meant the end of the home weaving industry. Workers moved *en-masse* into the dank, over-warm, unhealthy environments, thick with cotton fibres and dust, where disease ran rife, where the dirt fibrosed their lungs, driving them into early graves. But they did so willingly, in exchange for permanent and steady employment. Blackburn became a major hub of the cotton industry, not just in the North West, and not just in the United Kingdom, but in the world thanks to these fledgling entrepreneurs who became obscenely rich. They worked their employees hard and to the death; women looked prematurely old, men died of lung disease; and children were employed to service the machines as they worked. And yet, the jobs in the mills were seen as prestigious, and desirable. They paid well and the bosses encouraged loyalty by catering to their workers' every need, building houses and parks, hospitals, alms houses and schools. They charged low rent in times of plenty, and sometimes no rent when times were hard. They allowed decrepit and retired workers to stay on in their houses until the grave beckoned instead of evicting them. They fostered pride, pride in the mill, the town, the country, the Empire, building monuments to their conceit for all to admire. Darwen, for example, became home to the tallest chimney in the world, and it towers still, strangely beautiful with its harsh, industrial lines. But, in return for their munificence, they expected absolute obedience.

When education was made compulsory by government, it was encouraged that children should, after the age of 12 years, opt to be educated only part time, and work the rest of the week, the so-called 'half-timers'. As emancipation increased, employees were expected to vote in the same way as their bosses, and so whole districts voted liberal or conservative at the whim of the local Millocrat. The Labour movement, so important in the history of improving workers' rights and working conditions, took no real hold until the 20th Century because it was felt they were not needed. Support for workers' rights was rewarded with ingratitude of an enormous and unimaginable degree by the working class, its proponents being chased out of the district. This is not to say that the workers were completely passive. When they felt they were treated badly, they would stand together. In some cases, there were rampaging mobs, resulting in troops taking to the streets. Although some technocrats had to flee for their lives from burning houses, the disturbances usually evaporated as quickly as they started, and only gained a few paltry concessions in return for the imprisonment or deportation of the ringleaders. There were riots that resulted from the introduction of the *Spinning Jenny* automated loom by a minor manufacturer called Peel. Peel's son, Robert, would become an MP and eventually Prime Minister, and would be credited with the creation of that other British invention, the full-time professional police force. Constables are still referred to as "Bobbies" in his honour to this day.

The police in Blackburn were initially based in a Regency style building in Lord Street, with a gaol in the basement, now long demolished and replaced with a bypass. The three-story building housed a small, but innovative and dynamic police force which played a role in developing police procedures and forensics across the country. Two cases in the force's history stand out in particular through the gloomy annals of human violence.

On 28th March 1876 the Blackburn Constabulary was mobilised after one James Holland reported that his daughter, seven-year-old Emily Agnes, had vanished. She had last been seen leaving St Alban's school, telling her friends that she was not going straight home to Birley Street, but instead was going to run some errands for a 'nice man'. The search, which included the distribution of hundreds of handbills, was fruitless. Two days later, a labourer informed PC Raston that he had discovered some bloodied bundles in

Bastwell Field. These were found to contain body parts of a dissected young girl. Later that day, in Lower Cunliffe, her legs were found stuffed down a common drain. All the body segments were wrapped in the same edition of the *Preston Herald*. A post mortem concluded that the child had been sexually assaulted, but also identified an important clue: the body was covered in many, many different types of hair. Attention therefore focussed on two local barber's shops near the child's school. One was owned by Denis Whitehead, the other by father of three William Fish. The first search of the premises by Superintendent Eastwood, and detectives Holden and Stuart found nothing, except that Fish's shop contained a collection of newspapers. Four issues of the *Preston Herald*, corresponding to those which wrapped the corpse, were missing, used, Fish claimed, to stoke the fire. No further progress was made until April, when Chief Constable Potts was approached by local painter, Pete Taylor. Taylor had two dogs, a Spaniel and a half-breed Pointer/Bloodhound, whom he believed would be able to find the child's killer. On 16th April, Easter Sunday, after searching the sites where the body had been found, the hounds were taken to Whitehead's shop, with no result. They then moved on to Fish's workplace in Moss Street. Fish sat silently as the dogs padded around his shop, howling and snuffing at the chimney in the back kitchen. Under the direction of Superintendent Eastwood and Detective Livesey, Taylor reached up the flue and when he withdrew his hand, he held tiny fragments of burnt skull and jawbone. The skull still had wisps of brown hair attached.

Fish was arrested, stating only that he was innocent. The next day, the fireplace was entirely dismantled, and further fragments of skull and arm bones were retrieved. On Friday

21st April, Fish was formally charged in Court, where his own eventual admission of guilt was furnished as evidence against him. In his statement, he detailed how, just after 5 pm he saw Emily Holland passing his shop. Seemingly on the spur of the moment, he asked her to get a half ounce of snout for him from Cox's tobacconist up the road. When she returned, he enticed her upstairs to the front bedroom. By his own admission he 'tried to abuse her', and then cut her throat. He dismembered her downstairs and burnt the remainder after scattering her across the district. The miserable Fish had to be smuggled to safety to avoid a lynch mob. Little good it did him. He was found guilty and sentenced to death by hanging. It was traditional after such a sentence for some good-hearted worthy to at least plead for mercy for the guilty man. No such request was received on his behalf, and he was quite rightly executed in August 1876 at Kirkdale Gaol. No doubt the world was a better place without him.

This case was a national sensation, not only because it involved the grisly murder of an innocent, but because it was the first successful recorded use of dogs by a police force to catch a murderer. The whole sorry story was memorialised, as was popular and customary at the time in Victorian England, in a particularly lurid and graphic ballad.

20 years later, another child disappearance also ended tragically. Alice Barnes, 9, had last been seen standing on a bridge in Witton Park having helped herd her father Edward's cows into a field along with her sister Mary and friend Elizabeth Riding. The girls split up, but Alice never returned home. A short time later, Elizabeth's brother, Harry, was terrified by the sight of a running man, who threw a bundle over a wall. Harry asked a local woman,

Widow Hindle, to investigate. The discarded bundle was, of course, Alice's body.

The crime scene was hopelessly compromised by the time the police had arrived, but the investigators became very interested in the imprint of an unusually nailed boot found near the body. In those days, the nailing on the sole was unique, as good as a fingerprint, and allowed them to identify the cobbler responsible, who in turn was eventually able to confirm the owner when shown a drawing and a plaster cast of the print. It is this innovation that made it one of the seminal cases of early forensic investigation

In the meantime, more witnesses had come forward, and the police had been able to trace the running man's movements. However, many of these witnesses were children, and the forces of law and order were heavily reliant on both Harry and a young girl who claimed to have seen a man she regarded as 'not very promising' in the vicinity at the time

After several false leads, attention settled on ex-soldier and casual labourer Cross Duckworth. His alibi did not stack up, and it was noted by one witness that on the day of the murder he had changed his clothes without clear reason. There was little proper evidence against him, and none to show that Duckworth was either the man seen lurking in the park, or the man who was later seen running. Neither was there any proof that the boot-print, which was shown to match Duckworth's footwear, belonged to the man who had actually murdered Alice. However, a medical examination determined that Alice had died from choking on a distinctive handkerchief which had been forced into her mouth, which was thought to be similar to one that Duckworth sported.

At the trial, the children were not reliably able to identify the suspect, and witnesses were either led, if their evidence was against him, or had their evidence dismissed if it were in his favour. Duckworth was found guilty and was inevitably sentenced to death. However, this time there was enough concern about the safety of his conviction for local trade unions to write formally to the Home Secretary asking for the sentence to be commuted to life imprisonment. Despite this, Duckworth was executed in January 1893, on a snowy morning, publicly protesting his innocence until the end. However, it appears that Duckworth did confess to accidentally killing Alice to the Reverend who was present at his execution, although this was not uncovered until many, many years later.

Terrible crimes, but Victorian times were hard, and there were other matters to deal with. The town continued to grow around the blooming cotton mills, which were a source of employment and fortune, a driver of expansion, but they were also a hotbed of suppressed emotion. Long working days and weeks with whole streets of families working and living in close proximity made the mills a claustrophobic cauldron of sensitivities that occasionally spilled over, and there are many tales of tragedy. The most poignant occurred on 20th May 1912, a month after the Titanic went to its watery grave. Alice Beetham, a beautiful girl of 18, who was a weaver at the Jubilee Mill, Gate Street, Blackburn, walked into work as usual. She had been going out with a young man, Arthur Birkett, a workmate, but Alice had wider ambitions than those of worker, wife, mother, widow. Feeling that better things might be on the horizon, but not sure what, she had allowed the relationship with Arthur to end. Arthur was devastated, and blamed her father for disapproving of him, though Alice had said he was too 'passionate'. On the dread day, colleagues commented on how glum the young man looked, but he continued to work as usual, a silent, looming presence. During the scheduled breakfast break, Arthur went to a nearby shop and bought a razor for 1s 6d. The shopkeeper noted nothing remarkable, and described him as a seemingly ordinary, quiet young man. As Alice strode, carefree, across the musty work's floor, Arthur grabbed her from behind and quickly cut her throat nearly to the bone in front of all her friends. Her blood had barely hit the ground before he, rather ineffectually, turned the razor on himself. So quickly had the crime been committed that witnesses at first did not register what had happened, some thinking that Alice had fainted when Arthur had tried to kiss her. It was only the spreading pool of scarlet spray that alerted the fellow workers to the unfolding drama.

Despite his repeated requests, Arthur's life was saved by local doctors. When he had recovered, he was then tried, found guilty and sentenced to death. In a moving letter to his mother, he expressed his wish to die and be with Alice again. 'There is none like Alice to me,' he lamented. Despite a petition for clemency, supported vocally by Alice's poor mother, Arthur was hung by the neck until dead at Strangeways on July 23rd.

This sorry tale was one of many, sparked in part by the close and stressful working conditions sponsored by the mill owners. The Cotton Millionaires used and exhausted their workers and achieved in return wealth beyond the dreams of avarice, but their reign although significant, was astonishingly short. They built grand edifices, such as the gothic Town Hall that overlooked the town square and its many market stalls, bustling with vendors; the arcades housing shops full of treats and luxuries; the system of trams that ran through the town to the suburbs, like veins. Their wealth trickled down to the merchants and workers and lower classes as they grew incomprehensibly rich. Then, virtually overnight, they vanished, like dew in the dawn, leaving the town bereft and virtually bankrupt. Witton Park, the almost 500-acre estate that was home to the stately home built by the Fielden family in 1800 illustrates the brief but spectacular reign of these proto-capitalists.

The Fieldens had started out as Yeoman farmers before riding the crest of the cotton weaving wave. Their wealth soon surpassed the landed gentry and they ended up representing Blackburn's interests as MPs, High Sheriffs and Mayors. In a demonstration of their immense fortune, they annexed, enclosed and demolished the village of Witton to build a great country house, with drives, and courtyards, and stables, outhouses and outlying farms. By 1900, though the house was empty for increasingly long periods of time, and the whole area was sold to Blackburn Corporation in 1946 when the upkeep became prohibitive. Derelict as it already was, the house was demolished in 1952. All that remains of this statement of power and influence is the outline of foundations, the occasional wall, traces of paths, carriageways and the steps that once led to elegant gardens. From 1800 to 1946, the sprawling house and gardens were a stark testament of the swift rise and precipitous fall of the national cotton industry, the state of the nation writ small.

Between 1900 and 1940, over 100 mills closed as the bosses coped with the falling revenues by selling their assets off, and fast. The town fell on hard times, and previously skilled workers who could have resigned from one mill and been immediately re-employed at another found themselves increasingly redundant. This slide into penury was accentuated by more global disasters, not least the international catastrophe of the 1914-18 War which decimated a generation of youth, who instead of being valuable workers ended up as fertiliser in the green fields of France and Belgium. The misplaced confidence that men would fight all the harder if they were standing shoulder to shoulder with their mates led to the creation of the so-called Pals Regiments. The result was that whole villages of menfolk joined up, trained and ultimately walked towards death together at the hands of German machine guns. Towns were left bereft of men, fathers, brothers, sons. Few houses did not have an empty seat at the table, or a black ribbon on a framed photograph. So heavily affected were the northern mill towns by this disaster that the doomed Accrington Pals have been written into folk history as a representation of noble, but futile, sacrifice made, but not suffered by, an uncaring, unqualified ruling class. Devastated as it was, the East Lancashire Regiment regenerated to become one of the most feared units in the British Army. No job too dirty, they went on to fight in almost every theatre of the First and Second World Wars. The East Lancashires for example were one of the last groups to leave the embattled beaches of Dunkirk, having fought a bitter rear-guard action to keep the Germans at bay. For their efforts, the regiment was awarded the freedom of the town in April 1948.

Industry took another hit in the 1930's when, as part of the non-violent campaign for independence, the Indian nation boycotted British cotton. MPs, terrified by the rise of a militant working class, and the devastation that the failure of the cotton industry could bring, invited the movement's leader Mahatma Ghandi to Lancashire to see the hardship that resulted. He toured several towns, including Blackburn and Darwen, witnessing the poverty suffered by the locals who flocked to see him first-hand. It broke his heart, but not his spirit or cause. Poor as the English millworkers were, the deprivation suffered by his countrymen under the British yoke was worse, he said. Far from resenting him, the Lancastrians took the funny little man with the horn-rimmed spectacles to their hearts, treating him like a folk hero, a friend to the working classes, much to the alarm of the capitalist elite. So popular was the Mahatma that he is immortalised in ironwork railings at Blackburn train station.

Despite its decline, Blackburn remained such an important engine of the British economy that it was noted as a target by the Nazi Luftwaffe in the Second Great War. Pilots were given maps specifically highlighting areas of strategic interest. Fortunately, Blackburn was hit only once, leading to the devastation of Ainsworth Street, behind the Town Hall, and the death of two civilians. The Germans preferred to concentrate on fatter targets.

The Second War ended, and all too briefly prosperity returned, before another financial winter fell. In the wave of post war relief, austerity and the feeling that nothing, *nothing,* could surely be the same again, came a determination that the promises made after the *first* war to the working men and women should be met. A landslide Labour Party victory in the first post-war election ousted a surprised Churchill and brought Blackburn its first female MP, the formidable and fiery red-haired Barbara, later Baroness, Castle who served from 1945 until 1979. Whilst not a native Lancastrian, she was one of those determined Northern women who made sure things ran the way she wanted by sheer force of will. Like the town she represented, she was stoical, fierce, grim, and indefatigable.

And so, here we are at last, arriving in the mid-twentieth century, having all too briefly charted the decades of a town, deceptively unimportant, but at the same time disproportionately influential, a hub around which history whorled; home to a hardened breed of people, who fought fate, time, each other and mortality with an unrelenting grim determination. There is Blackburn, squatting serenely, malevolently, in the greenery of a scarred and gouged glen, a town of contrasts and contradictions, of bitterness and glory. There is the Town Hall, scowling over the marketplace. There, overshadowing it, the towering, arched clock with the golden ball that ascended a pole at noon, descending again at 1pm, in time with a cannon shot that would act as a visual and audible signal that mill worker's lunch break was over. There are the mills themselves, sign of innovation and industry, still kicking and screaming in their death throes. There is the commercial centre, including the glass roofed, cast iron Thwaites' Arcade, home to over twenty-two shops, joining the industrial and commercial arteries of the metropolis. One of the last towns to have trams, they scuttle like beetles through its byways, back and forth, back and forth, crowded with commuters, workers, lovers as they travel between the optimistically but misleadingly named districts of Waterfall, Paradise and Cherry Tree. There it is, Cottontown. Spreading out before us, nestled in the heart of a rugged valley, its chimneys stretching by the hundreds up into the sky, belching smoke and flame and fumes and gas in a never-ending cloud of scud and gloom that coated brick, and slate and lung.

Thousands of households sweltering in a constant muggy broth of smog. Cottontown, the legend, the throbbing engine of Empire, the master, the mistress, the whore, the mother. Cottontown, the heart, the murderous beating heart, of darkness.

Chapter 2

The Noble Guardian

Blackburn, Lancashire
June – November 1935

The traditional image of the slightly dullard British Bobby, adherent to strict rules, unimaginative and jobsworth, immortalised as Enid Blyton's PC Plod, was in most cases not representative of the kind of man, and it was almost exclusively men, who fulfilled the role. Dedicated to local service, the maintenance of order, and the prevention of crime, they were paid relatively little, and on duty 24 hours. In 1935, an exceptional example of this bulldog breed was due to face one of the biggest challenges of his career.

June 1935 was a month of harsh meteorological contrasts. A bright and warm May had drifted into an

19

overcast and violent weather system, with excessive rain, unrest and even flooding. Then, at the end of the month, the clouds broke, and temperatures soared to 88°F in central Manchester, and violent thunderstorms erupted to herald the traditional official end of the Great British Summer.

The weather reflected the mood of the country. In June, MacDonald, exhausted from domestic unrest and the threat of Nazi military expansionism, stepped down as Prime Minister, but extraordinarily, remained in the Cabinet under the Premiership of his colleague, Stanley Baldwin. A troublesome, rebellious and fractious elderly backbencher called Winston Churchill was once again side-lined, perhaps, some speculated, being saved for greater things. At Court, George V celebrated his Jubilee, but began the slow, inexorable slide, towards death. Meantime, the prolonged economic depression was taking its toll on the cotton-based industries in the north west of England. But, the people of Blackburn had other, grislier, matters to distract them from the grind of everyday life. On the night of Sunday 30th June, the residents of John Bright Street patrolled the local area in a search for a missing 3-year-old child. Today, John Bright Street no longer exists, the site having been subsumed by industrial units. Back in 1935, it was a group of narrow, terraced houses, tall, thin, with front rooms that opened directly onto the road over a single step that the housewives would proudly, and obsessively, scour clean. They all had a small back yard, surrounded by a wall to guard the kingdom. Helen was the only daughter of the Charles Chester family, who lived at number 22. The only known public photograph of her shows a blonde, bob-haired toddler, fist in her mouth, as she stares hauntingly past the camera. Last seen by her mother playing a short distance away, Helen had not responded to calls to return home a brief time later. As she was most recently seen crossing the bridge over the nearby River Darwen, Police feared that she may have been swept away, and so a riverbank search took place long into the night.

During the search, a Mr Pickering became concerned about the whereabouts of his own daughter, Margaret. He called upon the Chester's neighbours, James and Edith Mills, who lived at number 24, as it was known that, although childless themselves, the couple were fond of children, and often gave them treats and allowed them to play around their house and yard. When Pickering asked Mills if he had seen his daughter, the girl bounded out of the kitchen to be given a relieved scolding by her father.

By Monday morning, however, Helen was still missing, and the Police announced their intention to search every house in John Bright Street. At 3pm the same day, Henry Ball noted thick, choking, greasy smoke containing smatterings of paper emerging from the Mills' chimney for a short period of time. Later that night, Thomas Farnworth who lived two doors away from the Chester's and next door to the Mills', locked up his yard, noticing nothing unusual. However, the next morning his wife saw a large parcel by the back door. White haired and almost cachexic in appearance, Farnworth first checked that the yard was still secure. He then approached the parcel, which was wrapped in pages 9-10 of the local newspaper. Unwrapping it, he found a quilt, and inside the quilt, tumbling onto the stone floor of his yard, was the barely recognisable torso of a child. The body had been dismembered and burnt in places almost to charcoal.

After recovering from his horror, Farnworth ran for the Police. As a crowd gathered, and as officers set up a rudimentary crime scene, Jim Mills popped his head over the wall and stated to all and sundry that he had noticed the parcel when he had looked out of his bedroom window at 5am. It is not clear what possessed him to speculate publicly about events, and it is even more of a conundrum as to why he was at all surprised at what happened next. Mills immediately found himself being interviewed by notables of the Police, including Superintendent Langley, and the Chief Constable himself, Cornelius George Looms.

Looms was one of those men who was a truly devoted public servant. Born in London in 1896, if he did not remember Queen Victoria's 60th Jubilee, he would certainly have recalled her death and funeral. Initially, he adopted that typical career for young Edwardian gentleman, a solicitor's clerk. This profession was interrupted, as were the paths of so many, by the advent of the First World War. Looms joined the fledgling Royal Flying Corps, and stayed on in its successor, the Royal Air Force, until 1920. He left London, and by 1922 he had started another career in the Salford City Police Force. It is not clear how Looms came to leave *the Smoke* for *the Dirty Old Town*, the sordid and grimy twin of the great industrial slum that was Manchester. However, he made the north west of England his home. A determined man, he was a sergeant by 1924, and by 1926 had made Inspector and married his wife, Mary, in Morecambe. They had one son, George, and by 1928, Looms had achieved the rank of Superintendent.

In 1932, his stratospheric career rise continued as he was selected from 39 candidates to be Chief Constable of the Blackburn Borough Constabulary. He was only 36 years old, but he proved to be a wise choice. He immediately commissioned an investigation into accidents across his patch, with a view to improving community safety. He also introduced a series of mini police stations and the new blue Police Boxes across the Borough. This allowed decentralisation of the force, meaning that officers did not have to return to the station for important communications or updates, improving the numbers of feet on the ground and the ability of officers to respond quickly to emergencies. In a period when many forces were desperately trying to recruit more officers despite budgetary restraints, Looms was actually able to develop his service whilst allowing officer numbers to fall by natural wastage. He was also heavily involved in the training of new generations of constables through his positions on the management boards of both the Lancashire and Yorkshire Police Training Centres and gave time to other worthy causes outside of crime detection and prevention. For example, he was a patron of the Northern Police Orphanage and Convalescent Home and worked tirelessly with the Police Athletic Association. A keen sportsman, he captained the Lancashire Police Cricket first XI and was in his own modest words a 'capable' golfer; although in the words of others he was 'crack'.

During the Second World War, he served as an ARP Warden in his spare time, and in 1943, he appears to have been drafted as a Lieutenant Colonel for 'special military service' —usually code for intelligence work-in North Africa and Sicily. This tour of duty was cut short after a year due to illness, and he returned home to continue his policing duties.

In 1950 he would be awarded the Police Distinguished Service Medal in the New Year's Honours list to add to the medal he had previously received from the Humanitarian Society for saving a man from the notoriously treacherous Morecombe Bay sands.

Contemporary photographs show him to be a solid, respectable man with a clipped moustache, always impeccably suited, always tied, occasionally in his full-dress uniform. Unless the pictures are from the murder scene, he is always smiling.

In 1935, though, Looms had been Chief Constable for only three years. This child murder was his first real public test, and one that he needed to pass to retain the confidence of the community. Professional, diligent, modest, compassionate and humane, Looms would have been acutely aware that this was not the only infant murder that the people of East Lancashire could recall. The terrible child murders of yesteryear were one thing, but only months before Looms had been appointed, another local child murder had been solved by his colleagues in the Lancashire Police. She had been killed in uncannily similar circumstances to her unfortunate predecessors. 6-year-old Naomi Ann Farnworth was missed from her home in Darwen, and a police search, which utilised the boy scouts, failed to find any evidence of what had happened. However, it was later reported that a local youth, Charles Cowle, 19, had been seen threatening another young girl, Doris Sharples. Cowle had spent all night participating in the search for Naomi when he was approached by the Police at his home in Kay Street where he lived with his parents, a few scant doors away from her home. Cowle was not bright, and gave several different accounts as to what happened, finally admitting that he had asked Naomi to get him some chips from Mrs Brumfitt's, which he then shared with her. Finally, he took the police upstairs in his house, pointed to a trunk and said 'She is in there. I strangled her.' The girl had indeed been throttled. Cowle's defence had been insanity, on the grounds that he was diagnosed as a mental defective after a previous attack on a two-year-old boy which had seen him sent to Reform School. It did no good, and Cowle was executed at Manchester on 18th May 1932. The Farnworths eventually moved out of the area, but the Cowles stayed on in Kay Street, silently mourning the death of their defective, murderous child. Judging that they had been punished enough, the neighbours enclosed them in a wall of silence, protecting them from the prying eyes and enquiries of outsiders.

Looms was therefore fully aware of the importance of this murder to the community and the public, and the pressure on him to get a quick result must have been enormous. In any event, it was only right that the horrific death gained his full, and undivided, attention.

Looms interviewed Mills himself, and initially he wanted to know why he, a retired man, was up so early. Mills replied that he had not slept well, because he was worried about the missing child. Not an unreasonable explanation in itself, but Looms then asked why had he not reported the suspicious parcel himself when he had first seen it? Mills responded that he had not known that it contained the body of the child. Looms then pointed out that even now no-one had confirmed that it was in fact Helen's body that had been found and wanted to know why Mills seemed so sure the child was dead. Mills said he just assumed so, because of all the police activity.

Mills became increasingly evasive as the interview progressed, and eventually Looms asked him why the fireplace was so damp when the fire itself was burning well. Mills stated that his wife had bathed in the kitchen earlier. Suspicious by now, Looms had the fire extinguished, and his men discovered it was lined with thick grease. They also found several pieces of what could be human bone, and some buttons similar to those on the blue coat that Helen had been wearing. Mills tried to pass the bones off as a piece of left-over mutton, and then as a rancid fish they had destroyed. However, Dr Bailey, the police surgeon, identified them as human. Further evidence was found in a wastepipe, and bloodstains were found in Mills' bedroom. The floor had been recently cleaned, which Mills admitted doing himself. The police also found a bloodstained scrap of paper containing a blonde hair, which Mills claimed must have come from his grey-haired wife. Further horrors were revealed in the bedroom Mrs Mills occupied, separate from her husband. As well as the other half of the quilt used to cover the body, they discovered fragments of charred thighbone in a drawer. Mills suggested that the quilt had been cut up and used as an ironing cloth some weeks before, but it was later shown to have only recently been halved; in addition, the rest of the newspaper used to wrap the body was found; and the remaining string used to tie the ghastly parcel was identified. In the outhouse, a length of chain that Helen had played with was discovered, and a fragment of cloth on a wall revealed that the package with its pitiful contents had been pushed over into Farnworth's yard from the Mills' side.

Looms was certain he had his man. Unfortunately, Mills appeared to have an alibi. He had visited a cousin in Coniston Road on the far side of Blackburn on the day of Helen's disappearance and had not left for home until 7:45

pm. Having stopped to listen to a political speech in the marketplace, he did not arrive home until somewhere between 8:30 and 8:45 pm. He had found Margaret Pickering in his kitchen but had not seen Helen Chester. Margaret seemed to support his story, saying that she had not seen Helen whilst she had been in the Mills' house.

Mrs Mills, however, was making her own statement to Superintendent Langley. Being deaf, there was a macabre comedic moment when Langley had to read it back to her by standing very close and bellowing in her ear. She claimed that after tea at 5pm her husband had gone out. The first she heard of Helen's disappearance was when Pickering called at 7:45. They went to bed, but she could not sleep, and she castigated her husband for not being out searching with the other men. On Monday they rose at 6am and Jim left the house not returning until about 5pm. At 7:30 am the next day, Jim had already been up some time. He had made breakfast and lit the fire, telling his wife that they had found 'little Helen's body' in next door's garden, and said that he had found the back gate to their yard unlocked. The details that she gave did not entirely tally with her husband's.

Helen's remains were examined by an eminent pathologist, Professor MacFall of Liverpool University, who concluded that she had died having been struck on the head with a hammer similar to the one found in Mills' house. The blow was most likely to have been deliberate. The bone fragments that had been recovered were identified as belonging to the body, which was positively identified as Helen's by comparing remaining hair to a lock kept by the dead girl's mother. The bloodstains found in the house were identified as human.

It seemed to be an open and shut case. Helen was dead, and she met her end in the Mills' house, where an attempt to destroy all trace of her had been made. Both the Mills' were charged with her murder. However, the case did not proceed as smoothly as it should have done. After they were charged, Mills yelled an instruction at his wife not to say another word, and from that point they both adopted a strategy of silence. No motive was discovered, as rumours of ill feeling between Mills and Chester were unfounded. Most damningly of all, Mills' alibi seemed to stand up. If the time of Helen's last sighting was accurate, and the time of his arrival home, as verified by Margaret Pickering, were correct, he could not have possibly killed her.

Helen Chester's funeral was a sensation. The whole town turned out, people queuing up for hours before the sad little procession travelled from St George's Free Church, Mill Hill to at Blackburn Cemetery. It was estimated that there were over 5000 mourners. Whatever the numbers, extra police had to be laid on to clear the way. There was a heart wrenching note on a bouquet from two of her little friends, which read:

'One of the sweetest flowers gathered before its time
But now a star of Jesus will forever shine'

Men as well as women wept openly and bitterly.

The Mills' trial began at Lancaster Castle on the 16th October 1935, with both parties separately represented, and both pleading not guilty.

The prosecution adopted the strategy of proposing that Helen had died at the hands of one of the Mills' in the presence of the other, and then that both had conspired to dispose of her body in a variety of ultimately inept ways. The death could not have been accidental, because it would have been admitted immediately, or help would have been sought. In essence, a sort of 'joint enterprise' of unlawful death and conspiracy to pervert the course of justice was proposed. Mr W Gorman defending Jim Mills adopted a defence that was somewhat novel: he was not present when Helen had died, but he had tried to dispose of the body. The incompetence of the aborted kitchen grate cremation and the woeful attempt at the concealment of Helen's remains over the neighbour's wall were the act of a distraught man shocked at finding a child's corpse in house, not a scheming murderer.

Mr G Blackledge representing Edith Mills did not attempt to show that Edith had not killed the child but adopted the defence that it could not be shown with certainty that Helen's death had not been an accident. In addition, because she was stone deaf, she may have been unaware that Helen had entered her house and would not have heard if she had done so and then been murdered by an unknown opportunistic third party.

After two hours, the Jury returned a guilty verdict. Both Mills and his wife were sentenced to death. Mills was taken to Liverpool jail, still declaring his innocence, whilst Edith was taken to Strangeways in Manchester. Both appealed their sentences. However, Mills then turned evidence against his wife, claiming that he had not spoken out before for fear of incriminating his beloved spouse. He denied being at home when Helen had died, of attempting to burn her corpse, or of even seeing her body at any stage. He did in a statement however, allege that Edith had been in poor mental health, and that on the day the body was found that she had sneaked into the back yard before he was up and about. The appeal Judges agreed that there was no evidence that he had been in the house when Helen met her end, and so on these grounds, and on technicalities related to the original Judge's summing up, his conviction was overturned. Mills walked from Court a free man, straight into the prowling press pack. Fortunately for him, relatives were waiting. They whisked him away to the train station, and there then followed a chase across Lancashire with the newspaper men hot on his heels. Mills doubled back on the trains at least once and was finally taken away in a hired car. One of his relatives made a vain appeal to the Press to leave him alone, as he had already 'suffered enough'. Following this episode, Jim Mills does not appear to have returned home, and his ultimate fate is currently lost in history. Edith's appeal was dismissed, however. She sat through the hearing not knowing that she had been abandoned by her husband, or what the final verdict was due to her deafness, until she was led out of the dock back to the cells. Due to the overall uncertainty as to the exact chain of events, Edith Mills' death sentence was later commuted to one of life imprisonment on November 28th. For her, life was to truly mean life. She is reported to have died peacefully of natural causes at HMP Holloway, London on 5th March 1936. It is not certain that she ever really knew what was going on.

In one way, Looms' investigation was a success. Two people *had* been found guilty of the girl's death, and although one had his sentence quashed, the other was destined to die in jail. It must have been of concern to the Chief Constable however that despite his personal intervention, it seemed that the killers had escaped the expected justice. Neither actually paid the ultimate penalty demanded by society, and in fact the family never received an explanation of how or why the poor girl met her death. Was it just a ghastly accident? Or had Edith Mills, in the grip of paranoid dementia, clubbed her to death with the hammer? Had Jim Mills, desperate to save his wife, been moved to desecrate the child's body in a deliberate attempt of concealment? Or had Edith done this without his knowledge whilst in the grip of some form of mania? Despite the good superficial result, there must have been a feeling of frustrating disappointment, anti-climax, of justice denied. Looms was a good man, and he liked doing a good job. It is therefore easy to believe that this case preyed upon his mind in his darkest moments; that he endlessly revisited those days wondering if there was anything else he could have done to allow Helen Chester to rest easier, or to allow her devastated family to sleep better. His only consolation perhaps would have been that he was unlikely to ever face such a hideous, unthinkable, *unspeakable* situation ever again during his career.

Of course, he was sadly, terribly wrong.

Chapter 3

The Blunt Instrument

Merseyside, London, Wales and Lancashire
1903-1958

In mid twentieth century Britain, a cinema audience would pay their 2 ½ d, buy popcorn and drinks, and shuffle to sit in the dark to watch the main feature and a B-movie. In-between, there would be adverts and a newsreel. The newsreel was a very important magazine programme, dealing with current events. In the days before the internet, and in a time when the majority of homes did not yet have a tv, cinema was not only a popular form of entertainment, but a way to stay abreast of what was happening in the world. *British Pathé* had been producing newsreels for decades, mini- documentaries designed to educate, inform and entertain. On 24th November 1958, as the audience waited in the shadows to watch David Niven in *Separate Tables* or Yul Brynner in *the Buccaneer*, the flickering newsreel entitled *Big Robberies Alarm Authorities'* detailed concern about a spate of payroll thefts in the capital. In those days, transactions were performed using real cash, and the money had to be transported to and fro in cartoon-like moneybags. Many firms used trusted taxi companies to make the cash runs and had fallen into a pattern of predictable regularity to perform these transfers. It was this predictability that made them easy targets. As usual, a cab would turn up and the unsuspecting accountants would step in, realising too late that they were being abducted. They would be taken to an empty yard, where the rest of the gang would beat and rob them. The violence involved in some of these crimes was truly sickening, and some firms had taken to walking the money to the bank surrounded by a gang of vigilantes. To illustrate this, the news item showed a bowler-hatted, pin-stripe suited businessman holding a large cash bag surrounded by huge navvies carrying shovels and pitchforks as they sucked on cigarettes and comically tried to look hardened, desperate and grim.

The newsreel reporter then widened the debate into the usefulness of corporal punishment as a deterrent to violent crime. Specifically, it was being questioned by the Government whether 'a taste of the Cat' —a lashing with a nine tailed whip- should be reintroduced to the penal code. Flogging with the flail, or birch rod, had been used during the 20th Century to punish those who had committed acts of violence; but was used much more liberally in Victorian times. As society became more humanitarian in outlook, the punishment slowly fell out of favour. It had been abandoned for women criminals in 1820, and public demonstrations had ceased after 1831. However, boys as young as 14 years could still be sentenced to up to 36 strokes. The punishment had been outlawed completely in 1948, but it was felt by some that this now allowed nefarious villains to ply their trades with impunity. In the film, the Home Secretary, Rab Butler, was asked why he was against flogging such hardened recidivists. He replied, 'Well originally flogging was done away with in 1861, that's about 100 years ago. It was kept for crimes of violence up till 1948, then it was abolished ...and since then the crimes of violence have actually gone down, and now they stand at less than they were in 1948'. He announced that police forces were actively recruiting officers, but that it was important that current resources were used more effectively. Some Government messages never change. The reporter asked whether it was 'efficient' to have officers assigned to traffic duties rather than dealing with 'proper crime', and Mr Butler replied testily that traffic offences were indeed proper crime and caused greater loss of life in London than anything else.

At this point, the film abruptly altered tone, and the shot changed to show a backlit, stocky man, who scornfully announced, 'You expect miracles!'

Off-screen, the interviewer asked, 'And whom might you be?' in the clipped, received pronunciation that was typical in those times. At this, the lights went up revealing a grinning, white haired but vigorous looking middle-aged man, who replied in a broad northern accent 'I'm John Capstick, Ex Chief Superintendent of CID.' Impressed, the interviewer referred to him as one of Scotland Yard's 'Big Five', and asked him why he had a problem with the Home Secretary's comments. Capstick replied bullishly, 'Well you know, thieves who commit violence, they should be flogged with the Cat, they understand that.... they much prefer a double sentence of imprisonment than the Cat O'Nine tails.'

Capstick glared intimidatingly straight down the camera lens, with the confident smile of a man who knows, just *knows*, that he is right. He had the experience to see these new-fangled liberal ideas for the nonsense they were, and Capstick wasted no time in sharing his opinion on what he believed to be a ludicrous approach to modern policing. The only language your modern, brutal criminal understood was violence, and, being cowardly thugs at heart, they responded better to a proper punishment like a thrashing than they did to a term of confinement in one the comfortable so-called prisons that the Government maintained. This was an opinion that Capstick had shared before, in his memoirs. He had often resorted to using 'Johnny Wood' as he referred to the Police Constable's regulation truncheon, not only in self-defence, but as a prophylactic and preventative measure. *Hit 'em hard, and hit 'em first* was his motto. Apart from robust, but measured, use of violence he also felt that the secret to good policing was being out on the street, not sat in an office driving a desk, and he had contempt for those in seniority who were leading the police force down a false path because they had very little experience of actually feeling criminal's collars. Of course, he had nothing against female officers, but he felt that their role was doing the filing and traffic duty, freeing up their male colleagues to do the real work.

By today's standards, these opinions are hardly credible. However, it is important to remember that he was a man of his time. John Capstick was an old school thief-taker. Obstinate, pugnacious, forthright, dogged, he earned his right to have his opinions and express them as if they were absolute fact through years of hard graft, convictions, undercover work and aggressive pro-active policing on the dirty and violent streets of London. Clearly, even when he retired, times were changing, and he was already a dinosaur. This is alas the fate of us all. But in his time, he had been a successful alpha predator with a keen understanding and knowledge of the criminal underworld, and was often appointed to go out of the capital to assist fellow officers across the country who were dealing with heinous crimes that were beyond their experience and resources. Capstick was reliable, dependable, and he got results. He had progressed to his level of seniority the hard way, and was both respectable, and respected. He was, by any measure, a "copper's copper".

Capstick was born in West Derby, Liverpool in 1903. His parents, John and Mary Jane, were middle class dairy farmers, who had sold up and moved to then affluent Aintree. Although he was a bit of a wild child, who ultimately rejected the family business, in his middle years he was seldom seen without his tweedy suit, a Lancastrian rose in his lapel, and his big-bowled pipe clamped between his teeth, looking every inch the rural farmer who had strayed into town on business. In those days, children were thrown into the world of employment at an incredibly early age and having worked on a milk round which took in both the local police station and Walton Prison, young John was on friendly terms with both law keepers and law breakers. But he had his eyes on the wider horizon, and he actually fulfilled the fantasy that dreamy young men have oft threatened: he ran away to sea. Stealing a suit from his older brother he signed on as a deckhand on a cargo ship to the Argentine. He looked back on this year as the period during which his future career was probably decided, as he had some experience with theft, the gifts he had bought his parents having been purloined by one of his messmates. When he found that the locker below his bunk was packed with bolts of cloth stolen from the cargo, the crew threatened to throw him overboard if he did not keep their secret. In Rosario, he lost his last packet of English cigarettes to a 'yellow skinned news vendor' whom he chased down and apprehended. On return to Liverpool, he took an apprenticeship at W.B Band & Co., a wholesale fruit merchant, with headquarters in Vernon St, behind Dale St Police Station. He became friendly with the local coppers, possibly because his obvious admiration amused them. His work took him down the docks, and he was able to see the pilfering that was rife. As it offended his sense of honour, he tipped off the Dale St officers who arrested a large gang of thieves. One of them said, 'Johnny you're the best undercover man we've got. As soon as you're old enough, you'll have to join the Force.'

In 1919, he recalled meeting an 'impressive and amazing' man. The so-called Professor Best was a famous phrenologist from the northern holiday resort of Blackpool. A successful career had seen him retire to the better off areas of Liverpool, but he still peddled his skills at exclusive dinner parties for 'half a crown a head'. Burly, with a flowing silver mane and formidable eyebrows, augmented by a dark suit and silk lined cape, the 70 year old vaudevillian was offered the young John's skull to demonstrate his prognosticative powers at a dinner that had been organised by his mother. She was hoping, given his previous sea-going adventures, that a respectable career in the Merchant or Royal Navy might be proposed. To her dismay, the

Professor felt her boy's bumps, and after a period of thought, announced 'Madam, your son will either be a Great Detective, or a Great Thief!'

The fates were therefore determining the future for young John Capstick. All that was required now was that last roll of the dice that would set him on his path. That final push came in 1925.

Capstick always said that he would have probably ended up as a Liverpool copper if his chum Jimmy Robertson, a commercial traveller, had not suggested that the north was an employment dead-end and they should travel to London to look for work. Arriving at Euston with only a few shillings in their pockets, the first thing they saw was a recruitment poster for the Metropolitan Police. If accepted as a potential recruit, the young men would receive room and board, and, more importantly, £3 a week. Capstick reckoned that would do whilst he looked for a place in Covent Garden's markets. Jimmy failed the medical for being 8lb underweight, but Capstick, with his stocky but trim build was immediately accepted and was given a bed at The Police Institute, No 1 Adelphi Terrace. It was dirty, vermin-ridden and was home to ten recruits who were allowed one straw mattress and two blankets each.

After returning to Liverpool to work his two weeks' notice at the fruit business with Jimmy in tow, determined to bulk his weight up, he returned to London, taking a place at the temporary training school at Kennington Lane Police station, Elephant and Castle. Six weeks later, on his 22nd birthday, he graduated. Constable Capstick, PC402 of E Division, Warrant Card Number 114312, was assigned to the iconic Bow Street Station.

The Cottontown Killer

The criminals of the period between the wars are not as romanticised as the post Second World War era, with its celebrated and fashionable gangster wannabes who hung out with starlets, laundering money through their exotic nightclubs, thinking up their next blag whilst planning a retirement to the *Costa Del Crime*. The 'tween war criminals were steel men, hardened in the fire of the most terrible conflict. They were ruthless, brutal, dehumanised and had access to a supply of weaponry matched only by the bleakness of their consciences. Many of them would stop at nothing to make a quick bundle, and for some, murder was committed as casually as swatting a fly. The East End in particular had always been a nest for violent thuggery, and mobsters like the notorious Jack 'Spot' Comer, Billy Hill and 'Darby' Sabini ruled the London Underworld mercilessly.

It is worth giving a few brief examples of the type of man Capstick would have come across as a young, beat copper, as it speaks eloquently as to the kind of detective he became. For example, there was former Chief Constable Fred Wensley, who in his youth had pounded the streets of Whitechapel in the hunt for Jack the Ripper. Like all the London constables of the time, he was made to patrol with bicycle inner tubes stuck to his boots to silence the sound of hobnails, in order to give him the 'edge' should he ever actually have had a chance to sneak up on the sadist. He recounted in his memoirs how, as a constable, he apprehended double killer William Seaman after engaging him in rooftop hand to hand combat following a breath-taking chase. Seaman was consequently part of a notorious triple hanging which took place at Newgate on 9th June 1896. He shared the gallows with murderers Fowler and Milsom, and took his final journey placed between them, as hangman

Billington feared a repeat of the scene that had occurred in the Court during their trial. When he found out that Fowler had turned Queen's Evidence against him in an ultimately futile attempt to obtain clemency, Milsom leapt from the dock and attempted to throttle his cowardly co-defendant in full view of the Judge, the police and the prison guards. Realising why he had been placed thus, Seaman's last words before the trapdoor opened were reportedly 'This is the first time in my life that I've ever been the bloody peacemaker.' This, then, was the quality of the soulless men who frequented the London underworld. It can be taken that four years of a war that had scoured Europe had not improved their temperament any, as a ghoulish incident which occurred only two years after Capstick joined the Met illustrated. Mainly forgotten nowadays, the callous killing of PC George Gutteridge shocked the nation, and lead to what is widely regarded as the first 'trial by media'.

Somewhere after 3:30am On Tuesday 27th September 1927, Gutteridge stopped a car which was behaving suspiciously on the Chipping Ongar Road, Essex. He was not to know that it had just been stolen from a local doctor by the name of Lovell. A blue, four-seater Morris-Cowley tourer, index number TW6120, it was driven by two men, whose faces were hidden in the twilight. Unsuspectingly, he approached the vehicle, licking his pencil whilst he took his notebook from his breast pocket as he prepared to take down some details by the light of the car headlamps. Gutteridge leaned into the open window, and was shot point blank twice in the head. Staggering backwards, he collapsed, slumping against the roadside milestone, the unused pencil still in his hand. The murderer coolly stepped from the car, stood over him and, muttering 'What are you looking at me like that for?' shot out his eyes as he sat dying. These may have been the last words that Gutteridge ever heard. It was some time before he was found by his colleagues and the manhunt began, by which time the killers had escaped the area.

The search moved to London when the car was later found abandoned in Brixton, with a tell-tale fatal bullet casing under the passenger seat, and bloodstains on the running board. However, the investigation stalled until 1928 when Frederick Browne, whose real name was Leo Brown, a known criminal, was found in the possession of another stolen vehicle; the registration plates of different car that had been fenced and taken to Sheffield; and the proceeds of other locally committed crimes. A number of guns were found on his premises, one of which was shown to have killed Gutteridge. A large assortment of ammunition was also discovered, along with a frightening balaclava type mask, which had been knitted for his 'work' by his loving wife. Browne's known associate, Irish-Scotsman William Kennedy, went on the run, but was arrested in Liverpool. Whilst apprehended, he tried to shoot a police officer who was only saved because in his haste, Kennedy had left the safety on.

Browne always claimed his innocence, saying that Kennedy had given him the fatal weapon to store. Kennedy, however, said that he and Browne had stolen the car together, and that it was Browne who had murdered Gutteridge. Kennedy's written confession was released to the press and widely circulated before the trial began, causing a feeding frenzy and, some said, compromising their chance of a fair trial. For his part, Browne always denied being at the crime scene, and his defence consisted of defiant demands for the prosecution to 'prove it!' Kennedy gave no evidence at all, other than to submit through his barrister that his confession was fabricated. They were found guilty and hung together in 1928.

The East End of London was full of such men, and Capstick knew that his reputation would be made or broken on those mean streets. The hard drinking, poverty stricken east-enders were not above baiting policemen, and If he failed to meet any challenge in the early days, he would be finished as a copper, a laughingstock. He was dismayed to find that his regulation boots were stolen from inside the police station, but he turned this setback into an advantage. Instead of boots, he wore running shoes, which he disguised by wearing his uniform trousers long. This made him light on his toes, and a formidable pursuer. After being ambushed and beaten on a solo foot patrol, he realised that a copper's best weapons were his wits, and his baton. He went everywhere in future with his thumb through the leather loop, so as to draw it quicker in a crisis. Officers were taught to deploy the truncheon onto the assailant's shoulder as a deterrent. Capstick found that the side of the head, over the ear, was much more effective.

Eventually he made his name by settling razor and fist fights at Tommy Farmer's doss house. Once, he ended a brawl at *the Empress'* by dragging an enormous Irishman to the station by his moustache. Strangely, this Irishman later joined the RUC, and he and Capstick became both colleagues, and friends. Capstick built his stature on these narrow streets, patrolling through his Bow Street Manor, Covent Garden, Waterloo Bridge, Fleet Street, Seven Dials and the warrens of slums at the Ripper himself had once walked. He never ran from a fight, and he never turned his back on a crime. He gained a fearsome reputation amongst his colleagues, and the denizens of the underworld referred to him respectfully as *Charlie Artful*, reflecting his raw, native cunning. He of course received several commendations for his arrests and conduct. When Jimmy Robinson returned to enlist, having finally made the weight grade, they both arrested a couple of shop breakers, even though Jimmy was not actually a warranted officer at the time, a fact the Court conveniently chose to overlook.

Capstick always said that it was his education at the university of hard knocks as a famed Bow Street Runner that catapulted his career upwards. Ambitious, successful, brave to the point of foolhardiness, rugged, devil-may-care, Capstick spent only a year in uniform before graduating to the CID. Within seven years, he was one of the youngest Detective Sergeants in the country. Shortly afterwards, Capstick was recruited to the famous Metropolitan Police Flying Squad- the notorious *Sweeney* (named for the rhyming slang 'Sweeney Todd')- under the command of Alf Dance. This team of undercover, plain clothed officers coupled with their mobile radio units and fast cars were the police 'special forces' against crime. A major part of the Squad's role was crime prevention, which in many cases seemed to consist of turning up at a rogue's funeral and intimidating his friends and colleagues. Alf and his brother Squibs were masters of disguise, and Squibs particularly would spend days or weeks undercover, chumming up to known criminals who would treat him as one of their own and eventually regret confiding in him at His Majesty's Pleasure.

After promotion to Detective Inspector, Capstick left the Squad temporarily, and was assigned to a variety of inquiries. He solved the first of his many murder cases during the second war. His wife had been evacuated, and he was living in digs above the Charing Cross Hotel, when he was roused to find that popular publican Morrie Scholman of the of the Covent Garden *Coach and Horses* had been shot through the head at close quarters.

His past experience as a fruitier allowed him to converse with the Covent Garden stallholders in their own terms, and, having developed an excellent rapport over the years, they fed him good information. They identified a running soldier, his face covered in a muffler, as the likely perpetrator. Sadly, at that time, London was of course full of servicemen of all nationalities. How then to find one amongst so many? Capstick was not a believer in procrastination and took the initiative. He decided to contact the local Provost, commandeered a battalion of Redcaps, rounded up every soldier billeted within a one-mile radius of the murder of whatever nationality, and took them all to Bow Street Station for interviewing. They soon identified one absentee, Canadian Lance Corporal James Caie Forbes McCallum, and found him in bed with his girlfriend. He had an arm wound, which, he confessed had occurred when he had attempted to rob Scholman. In the struggle that ensued, his gun went off accidentally, and the bullet passed through his arm into Scholman's head. Previously of good character, the soldier was sentenced to death, but this was eventually commuted, and he spent several years in jail in Canada.

Capstick re-joined *the Sweeney* during an initiative designed to break the Black Market that thrived in the blackout of the Blitz. In a period he described as '90% work and 10% leisure', he formed his own team of six men and tackled the gangs head on, tirelessly feeling the collars of scores of criminals. No tip no matter how trivial went un-investigated, and any possibility of an impending crime was staked out, sometimes by officers in ridiculous wigs who in the dark were taken as women entertaining their lovers. Many of the men they arrested were deserters from the forces, ruthless and trained in killing, who, without ration books, had no means of supporting themselves other than crime. The police however were equally hardened and did not often bother with a polite request to accompany them to the station, or the legal niceties of a search warrant. One glorious Christmas Day raid saw three prisoners spending the nativity in hospital. On other occasions, Capstick and his team would brazenly walk into a crime scene pretending to be part of the gang before seizing their prey, which usually involved close combat. On another memorable occasion, Capstick even took his wife Babs on a stake-out before proceeding on to a night out after the arrests had been made.

In 1946, the notorious Ghost Squad was formed. Capstick was placed in command of this group of elite-and ruthless- officers whose job was to take the war on crime into the enemy's camp. The Ghost Squad's main function was to gather intelligence of potential crime and criminals by any means, and then to pass this on to local forces who would make the arrests. Capstick and his men would not get credit, or take part in the later Court case, remaining completely invisible. *Ghosts*. His hand-picked men included Nobby Clark, who 'punched like a mule's kick'; John Gosling, the 'Suffolk Giant with the perennial trilby'; Matt Brinnand, the 'expert man-hunter'; and George Burton, who sang at pub concerts and thereby gathered his information from the idle chatter that occurred afterwards.

Within a year, 157 men had been arrested for stealing or handling stolen goods; and thousands of pounds worth of property had been recovered. The officers sailed close to the legal wind on many occasions and were not averse to methods that could be regarded as entrapment. But the men they were up against were murderous and ruthless, and the occasional women gangs that crossed his path, he remembered, were just as bad.

Capstick later moved from Serious Crime, to the Murder Squad, an assignment that took him around the country. His first case as a travelling Scotland Yard detective was the killing of a Glamorgan woman, known as 'Rachael the Washerwoman', from Wattstown. It was never clear if the 76-year-old was a widow as she claimed, or if she had been deserted by her husband, but she scraped a living by taking in laundry. At 11:20pm on 12th October 1947 her beaten body was found lying in the street. The Chief Constable called Scotland Yard and Capstick and his sidekick 'Geordie' Stoneman, who sported a flamboyant RAF moustache, were dispatched. Arriving the next day, after driving through the darkness of the Rhondda Valley to the occasional, distant accompaniment of massed male voice choirs which could be heard intermittently drifting on the wind from the many local chapels, they examined the poor woman's remains. The key in her hand testified that she had met her end as she had opened her own front door.

Capstick was a big believer in the concept of the local beat Bobby as a source of intelligence, in this case a PC Steve Henton. Henton immediately provided him with two names on a piece of paper. One was a man found to have a longstanding quarrel with the woman. The other was local tearaway Evan Haydn Evans, known locally as Blackie because of his dark, dark hair. It then became known that Rachael was seen arguing with a man wearing a brown suit answering Evans' description outside the local pub.

Evans lived with his parents on a farm atop a rugged hill, and the next day, the team went up to pay him a visit. His behaviour immediately aroused suspicion when he tried to stop his mother giving the police a pair of highly polished black shoes. Evans wore a blue suit for the subsequent interview, claiming that he had never owned a brown one.

After a period of interrogation, he admitted having words with the washerwoman after she had called him a 'filthy pig'. He denied harming her at all. However, after finally being taken into custody, Evans broke down and admitted that he had drunkenly stumbled into the woman on his way home from the pub as she opened her door. She threatened to call the police on him, and, losing his temper, he hit and kicked her to the floor.

And yet, despite the confession, there was no blood on that blue suit. Witnesses insisted Evans had a brown one, and Capstick needed the proof to make the confession stick. The phenomenon of 'false confession', where a psychologically needy individual admitted to crimes that they had not committed, was not unknown. Although Capstick was convinced of Evans' guilt, he was not so desperate for a conviction that he would risk an innocent man taking the short walk to the long drop. Capstick and his team returned to search the Evans' home from top to bottom. Eventually, Mrs Evans' refusal to get off the single, drab settee gave them the clue. It turned out that Evans and his mother had hidden the missing brown suit inside the sofa. The clothes were heavily blood-stained, and the ferocity of the assault was evidenced by the fact that a piece of bone was found embedded in the cap. The defence tried to argue that the old lady had died accidentally after being punched, by banging her head on a flagstone, so that the death was manslaughter, not murder. The Judge and jury found the explanation not entirely convincing. Evans went to the gallows on 3rd February 1948.

So, there was Capstick, not a man to stand still when action was needed to get results, not afraid to get his hands dirty, a policeman's policeman, with a track record at solving vicious and brutal crimes. He was therefore a natural choice to send when eight weeks' after Evans' execution two boys were murderously attacked in Bolton, Lancashire. And it was his involvement in this next case that directly led to his trip to Blackburn the following month.

Chapter 4

Death on the Tracks

Farnworth, near Bolton, Lancashire
April-May 1948

The period between 1947 and 1949 would be one of extended drought, with higher than average temperatures. Early 1948 however would be mercurial in its climate. There would be months of torrential downpours, snow in Northumberland, and in April thunderstorms of such ferocity that two players in the Army Football World Cup final at Aldershot would be killed by errant lightning strikes. The match was abandoned, and because the score was drawn, the two teams involved shared the trophy, a typically pragmatic British end to a traumatic day. No doubt, the resolution of the tragic events also involved copious amounts of hot, sweet, milky tea. However, shocking these events were, they did not prevent hardy and resolute individuals meeting similar lightning-based deaths in Gloucestershire later in the same month

Perhaps the tumultuous weather was actually of some comfort to the British, who were in the midst of post war austerity, defined by Government enforced rationing of fuel and basic staples, and the stiff upper lip 'mend and make do' attitude so characteristic of this island race, particularly as world events after the destruction of the evil of Nazi Germany were not progressing as the politicians had promised. Clement Atlee's Labour Government had ousted Churchill in the post-war elections and was desperately trying to deliver on the promises it had made. The flagship policy of the creation of a National Health Service, free at the point of use, was finally on the verge of being instituted and would make an enormous long-term difference to the health of the public, who for the most part lived in poverty in slum areas of urban conurbations, or in the isolated rural outlands.

Disappointingly, though, the relaxation of food rationing was slow, and Atlee had been required to call upon the Army to break a 1947 dockworkers' strike that had held the country to ransom and left much needed meat rotting on the quayside. It was hoped, however, that the petrol ration might be eased later in the year, and that bread might become freely available completely. That funny little man Ghandi had found that his unique brand of passive-aggressive pacifism was no protection against assassination, and there was now a real danger that the sub-continent, recently in turmoil due to an enforced partition into separate nations, would descend into chaos. Many of those mill workers in the English north west industrial towns that had flocked the streets to see him when he had toured shed a tear at the loss of a man they regarded as a comrade in arms in the struggle against the rich and powerful. In the East, Uncle Joe Stalin was girding his loins for a round of Soviet expansionism that would on more than one occasion bring the world to the brink of nuclear war. Already the West's access to Berlin through the rail, road and canal links had been severed, and was being enforced by the military might of the Red Army. When a Soviet Yakovlev Yak-3 jet collided with, and downed, a British European Airways Vickers Viking 1B near RAF Gatow, killing all involved, it did not quite bring the world to the edge of destruction, although it certainly dropped the temperature of the Cold War by several more unwanted degrees as the Iron Curtain continued to fall across Europe.

Another reason why the weather was of interest was because Britain had agreed to host the first post war Olympics, in London. These would later be known as the 'austerity games'. It was anticipated that such a high-profile event would not only raise morale, distracting the public from the hum drum reality of life and from the fact that the sun was indeed finally setting on the once mighty British Empire, but would boost the economy, creating job and retail opportunities that could be readily exploited by *Great Britain PLC*, so it was important that the weather was fine.

It might have been grim to be an adult, but it was a good time to be a schoolboy. Providing that the War had not bombed you from your home, or taken your family, you could enjoy a degree of freedom that children today could only dream of. Certainly, discipline at home and at school was tight, even brutal. But this was the mythical 'golden age' of boyhood that newspaper editors and politicians hark back to time and time again, where simple experiences such as getting filthy in the comforting soot as a steam train passed hooting under a bridge, or watching Spitfires whirling in the blue sky overhead would be the height of pleasure; where the summer went on forever; and an impish youngster could while away the hours climbing trees, playing endless matches of cricket and football, or swimming in the quarry without fear; where the height of juvenile crime was a bit of apple scrumping, and where community policing meant that the local constable could give you a good natured a clip around the ear as a dose of crime prevention

On 12th April, two such jolly pals were amusing themselves by playing on the railway line at New Bury, Farnworth.

Today, New Bury is a suburb of nearby Bolton, a town on the outskirts of Manchester. In 1948, it was no more than a few streets, surrounded by rolling fields. The main line from Manchester Victoria, north to Clitheroe, still runs through Farnworth, but in post war Britain, the area was also criss-crossed with numerous branch lines, the veins of commerce, punctuated by tiny local little platforms. The importance of this rail network cannot be emphasised enough, and it is a matter of fact that the mere presence of a train line changed the nature of the landscape forever. For example, the industrial villages of Marsden, Hebson and Bradley in East Lancashire became collectively known by the name of the public house that was situated next to the local station and continue to rejoice in the name of *Nelson* to this day.

The Cottontown Killer

New Bury was served by Plodder Lane station. Plodder Lane itself ran from the west towards Farnworth, and New Bury was sandwiched into the streets bordered by Highfield Road which ran parallel to it. St James' Church and School bounded the south edge of the district, running next to the Bridgewater Collieries' Railway. The unimaginatively named Lower and Higher Streets joined Barton Road, which ran into Piggot Street, the eastern boundary. The rest of the area consisted of Blindsill Mill, at the end of the eponymous road; Century Mill; reservoirs; farms; and fields. Some of these thoroughfares which were reportedly little more than dirt tracks were bisected by George Street. The Church was nestled between some ancient terraced houses. A few more homes with memorably long entrance halls trickled along Highfield and Piggot Street and merged into the prefabs on Barton Road that had been built during the War. A scattering of family owned shops served the locality, rejoicing in colourful, evocative names such as *Hanbury's Grocery, Molly Fisher's Fish and Chips, Old Joe Clogger's, Morton's Shoe Repairs*, and *Guy Jones' Chemist*. Off one of the main streets squatted Eli Dyson's cotton spinning factory with its hundreds of looms. There was a Salvation Army Hall and a Post Office; and the public house, *the Spinner's Arms*, known colloquially as 'Mr Naylor's Pub' was the heart of this tight knit community. In the 20's the hamlet had its own 40-piece Jazz Band, based at the pub, led by local enthusiast Mr Butler. The prize-winning ensemble sadly did not survive its impresario's passing.

Just outside the village, David Lee, aged 9, and his school chum and neighbour, Quinten Smith, known as Jack, were scrambling along the embankments and defiles of the open fields and tracks, playing in the cool evening sun, despite the fact that the local adult population of Bolton were currently in the habit of warning their children about the perils of playing in isolated areas following a series of chilling events.

On 18th August 1944, 6-year-old Sheila Fox had been walking home from lessons at St James' Primary School when she went missing. She was last seen, laughing and giggling on the handlebars of a stranger's bicycle, telling her friends 'I'm going with the man'. Sheila was a fair haired, round faced angelic looking girl, with pink ribbons in her hair, described by a childhood friend as a 'quiet little thing'. She often played in the street with her sisters and other children. On the day she vanished forever, like dust on the wind, she was dressed in a distinctive blue floral frock, green coat and brown stockings with black shoes. It was theorised that she must have known the man on the bike, because she was shy, and would not voluntarily go off with people she did not know. According to the Lancashire CID crime despatch dated 22nd August 1944, the man on the *Roadster* model enamelled bicycle with distinctive upturned handlebars was about 5 feet 8 inches tall, 25 -30 years old, with a clear complexion, a long face, sharp features and a pointed chin. He had brown hair, and wore a blue suit, shirt and tie. Despite intensive investigations, her parents died without ever seeing her again, although every night, they reportedly left the front door on the latch in the vain hope that she might well, one day, just walk back in as if nothing had happened.

The police operation wound down without ever determining her fate or the identity of 'the man'. But sadly this was not the last offence against a child in New Bury.

12 months later, 6-year-old Patricia McKeown survived a stabbing attack in St James' Street. Yet again, the police were

unable to trace the attacker. Then, in March 1948, Brenda Hume was also attacked on her way to St James' school. She was tormented by a man with a knife who left her covered in cuts. Luckily, the attacker was seen and chased off by the headmaster of the school, Mr Bath. Sadly, Bath had a terrible limp and had to give up the chase as the attacker fled to Clegg's Lane and then the wider area.

Despite the large number of attacks occurring in such a small area, no suspects appear to have been arrested. As is the way of things, the inquiry into little Sheila's disappearance was never officially closed, and, based on information received, in 2001 the Greater Manchester police excavated the garden of a terraced house in Barton Road which had previously been the home of one Richard Ryan, deceased. In 1950 Ryan was convicted of rape; and in 1965 of the indecent assault of a child. The search found nothing, and Sheila is still, officially, a missing person rather than a murder victim. David Lee, later a retired gardener residing in nearby Bromley Cross, had lived a few doors down from Sheila on MacDonald Avenue. In later life he was interviewed for a local newspaper and recalled his memories of the young girl who had lived around the corner, and the horrifying events which were to unfold to him and Quinten on that glorious April evening.

Quinten who lived on Bradford Street, was David's best mate, and was known to be a live wire. During summer camping trips, for example, he would release the tent ground pegs for a laugh, and his friends would struggle out of the canvas to be greeted by his grinning, round face. Boys will always forever be boys. Quinten lived opposite the railway, and its pull was magnetic. This was their usual playground. After school on the fatal day the two lads scuttered around the meadows alongside the tracks, enjoying the evening sun, not really thinking about the warnings of their parents about past mysterious child assaults. Eventually, they decided to try out their scouting skills by the railway bridge. They collected and bundled some sticks and lit a couple of minor fires in the evening haze, watching as the smoke plumes drifted into the sky and dwindled into nothing. So absorbed were they in this activity, that they did not see the tall, thin stranger until he was upon them. David was later able to describe the man in nothing more than broad, unfocussed terms. 5ft 10 inches tall, with brown or greying hair, and a blue, zigzag patterned suit, black shoes and a spotty face. He looked at them disapprovingly and claimed to work for the railway. He told them that they had broken the law by playing near the tracks and setting fires. Arson was a very serious crime, and he had no option but to take them to the police. They would have to come with him.

Boys are naturally rebellious, but at that age they are also fearful of authority. No doubt thinking of how upset their parents would be when they found out about their naughtiness, they walked ahead of the man as he took them a bit further along the track. Then he ordered them to lie down.

David was naturally vague about what happened next, and it was never fully reported in the local papers. The details of the crime are held in the UK National Archive but are not due to be considered for release until at least 2028. Police interviews of the time only referred to the perpetrator as a dangerous sexual maniac, although it was emphasised in the papers that this had not been a sex attack.

David was assaulted first, and it is possible that Quinten intervened to allow his friend to escape. It is horrifying to think that the attack took place in full view of the houses that bordered the pastures. So near, so very far.

David had been stabbed in the chest, stomach and the groin. Despite his serious injuries, he staggered into a neighbouring street where he was found by a housewife as he attempted to crawl home. A search was started, and soon Quinten's partially naked battered body was discovered face down near the railway line, in a field off Plodder Lane. Like David, he had been stabbed multiple times with a small knife but had died after being battered with a blunt object. An unusual penknife was later found some distance from the scene, but there were no identifying factors or fingerprints that could link it to a perpetrator

Some local lads were playing football in a nearby field. They recalled being stunned into sick silence when the game was interrupted with news of Quinten's murder. Farnworth and Bolton became towns of fear. It was highly unlikely that such a small area would have bred two separate child killers, and so the locals and the papers made the obvious link to all the previous child attacks, concluding, not unreasonably, that there was a serial child murderer involved. It was widely believed that the killer lived in the area because of the degree of local knowledge shown, but the population did not want to believe that one of their own could be responsible for the terrible series of crimes. However, now no child was left alone. Parents took it in turn to escort groups of children to and from school and other activities. It was soon realised that black haired David Lee was particularly vulnerable. In the hospital as he was, he could be kept relatively safe. At some point however, he would have to return home, to the same streets prowled by the maniac, whom only he could identify. Thanks to the local gossip and the papers, the killer would know exactly where he lived, and how to find him. As a result, for over a year, David would have a police escort wherever he went.

The police were still being heavily criticised for failing to find the killer and attacker of Sheila Fox and the other young girls, and so help was called in from local forces, who supplied 110 officers to help with the search. One of those who pledged assistance was Cornelius Looms. A call was soon made to Scotland Yard, famous headquarters of the Metropolitan Police. The enviable resources of the Yard were made immediately available, and on 16th April 1948,

Geordie Stoneman and his imposing *Guv'nor*, Capstick, were sent to take over the inquiry. They immediately organised an extensive and thorough search and, on several occasions, Capstick released details to the press in anticipation of an arrest. Sadly, these leads came to nothing. For example, an agitated driver who had burst into a pub in Westhoughton on the day of the murder made himself known and was eliminated from the enquiries. Despite the firm belief that a local man was responsible, and a tiny, confined area to search, no real progress was being made at all. The discouraged officers even questioned the inmates of local psychiatric hospitals without success.

In his memoirs, Capstick only briefly mentions the investigation in Farnworth as a prologue for the horror that was yet to come. He describes how he and Stoneman, and the local forces worked 'around the clock, grudging every second snatched for a hasty meal or nap'. Thousands of men, women and children were questioned, and hundreds of miles of fields, and byways, and roads and streets were trawled for clues without result. The Yard's men co-ordinated the effort, but after a month, they were recalled to

London to give an update to the Top Brass. On the evening of 14th May 1948, as they sped on the train south through the grimy smokestacks of Manchester, failure hanging heavy on their shoulders, Capstick turned to Stoneman and said hopefully 'Thank God we'll get a full night's sleep'.

Later that evening, Capstick ate with his wife, and settled down to rest. He was completely done in and was immediately dead to the world. It seemed though that his head had hardly touched the pillow when the phone rang. Cursing as he realised it was only 4am, he trotted grumpily into the hall to take the call. What on Earth was so important that it could not wait until the morning? After a short conversation, Capstick returned in purposeful silence to his bedroom, and immediately started to get dressed.

Babs was a copper's wife and was used to the unusual and prolonged hours that they worked. However, this recall seemed to her to be beyond the Pale. 'Surely, they're not calling you back in?' she snapped, but her husband's reply had her making a hasty breakfast with a pasty face as he packed his bag. The call from the Yard had been prompted by Cornelius Looms. The killer it seemed had struck again, this time in Blackburn. Brazenly, a young girl had been stolen from an in-patient cot and murdered in the hospital grounds. As he bolted his meal and stepped into the Flying Squad car that had been despatched to take him to the 06:20 from Euston, Babs said 'Jack, this time you've got to get him. No matter what it takes.' Capstick nodded in reply, a curt bob of the head, his face pallid in the dark.

Her words must have echoed around Capstick's brain as he and Stoneman, who was carrying the 80 lb 'murder bag' containing all their kit, tried to grab fitful sleep on the north bound train. Get him, Jack. Get him, No Matter What it Takes. No. Matter. *What.*

Chapter 5

The Abolitionists

Great Britain
50 BC – 1948 AD

Britain only removed the death penalty from the statute book relatively recently, and there are still many who regret its' passing. The media are full of stories about those individuals who have committed heinous crimes, languishing for apparently ridiculously short periods of time at public expense in prisons allegedly little better than holiday camps, rather than paying the ultimate price for their murderous rages, even though hanging is probably 'too good for them' anyway. Despite the possibility of judicially ending the life of a wrongly convicted innocent, there are many bar-room pundits who think that the risk of a guilty killer walking free is the greater evil, and that, as espoused by the notorious Abbé Almaric, if you kill them all, then God will probably sort them out later. This simplified view overlooks the fact that a life sentence prisoner is released only on license, and can be hauled back into jail if they fail to keep to the terms of their release; and that there are still in the 21st century individuals who are controversially subject to a whole life imprisonment tariff, destined *never* to be released. More importantly, it is forgotten that the ultimate punishment was not always consistently, and as ruthlessly, applied as those in favour of it would like to believe.

For example, despite their admirably brutal tendencies, the Romans abolished the death penalty for their citizens. When there were attempts to re-instate it, none other than Cicero, the master of rhetoric, spoke against it. 'Far from us be the punishment of death, its ministers and its instruments!' he thundered, 'Remove them, not only from the actual operation on our bodies, but banish them from our eyes, our ears, our thoughts. For not only in the execution, but the apprehension, the existence, the very mention of these things, is disgraceful to a free man …!' In theory, throughout their Empire, any person could avoid a death sentence by proving merely that they were a Roman Citizen, much good that it did Cicero in the end. Barbarians, on the other hand, they happily slaughtered with alacrity, in many inventive and ingenious ways.

In the Anglo-Saxon era, the offer of financial compensation, so called *wergild,* could calm the aggrieved relatives of the victim sufficiently to allow the killer to live. Of course, these were times in which the average man, in order to survive to the ripe old age of thirty or forty, had to not only avoid disease but be prepared to bury a sword or dagger or axe in the body of a fellow being at frequent intervals. Therefore, it is possible that the practicalities of decimating the population by executing every killer had some sway on this position of financial compensation. Following the Norman invasion of 1066, the Conqueror virtually abolished the death penalty. This was not from an enlightened sense of mercy, but because the death of a man was a wasted economic resource. Instead, Normans favoured a graded series of mutilations as a highly visible and lasting deterrent to criminal behaviour, which, for example, included such terrible crimes as being away from the Lord's Manor without express permission. In addition, multiple degrading ways of carrying out the punishments waxed and waned in favour. Henry I re-introduced hanging as the preferred method of despatch. This involved merely hoisting the individual by the neck over any jutting branch; or the so called 'short drop' performed by simply kicking away a stool. Both methods resulted in the condemned gradually throttling to death. Cheap, efficient and able to be performed on an economically large scale, it was an immensely practical method of execution. Beheading was reserved for nobility, being the favour of a quick, clean death to avoid the humiliation of slow strangulation. The fitting fate for those who committed treason was the dreadful hanging, drawing and quartering: being suspended by the neck until *nearly* dead, then being cut down, disembowelled and having the vitals burned in front of their still living eyes, until the mercy of decapitation. The body would then be cut up and parboiled, the parts to be displayed at the four corners of the kingdom, the head to be preserved on a pole above London Bridge. Such was the ghastly fate of the

Gunpowder Plotters, for example. Burning alive on the other hand was the merciful punishment reserved for witches, heretics and other undesirables.

Whatever its form, capital punishment was usually carried out in public, making for a popular diversion from the grinding misery suffered by most of the population. There are reports of huge carnivals at public executions, with so many people attending that sometimes the large platforms built for the audience would collapse, causing injury and loss of life. Some towns would develop their own unique traditions of execution. Halifax, and many Scottish cities, for example, invested in a primitive version of the guillotine. As always, those in a position of privilege had options of avoiding execution that were not open to those who were the lowest born. For example, if one could prove they were a churchman, they could invoke the *Benefit of Clergy* and escape death. This was done by reciting key parts of the 51st Psalm, which became known as the 'neck verse' as a result. It's not clear how many people this quirk actually saved. In addition to the famous beheadings, the grotesque Henry VIII is reputed to have had 72,000 people hanged in various attempts to quell rebellion and preserve his dynasty. He also introduced the novel punishment of boiling alive for poisoners, who were regarded as particularly treacherous individuals.

The number of crimes punishable by capital sentences has both decreased and increased over the centuries. Contrary to popular belief, there were only about 40 capital crimes on the statute book in the supposedly uncivilised Middle Ages. This fell to 30 during the reign of Good Queen Bess. In the eighteenth century, however, the introduction of the so-called Bloody Code of 1723 more than doubled the misdemeanours for which death was the penalty. Another 60 were added during the reign of Mad King George III. These new capital statutes related mainly to the protection of the rights of the propertied class and their land and possessions from the growing dispossessed. In effect, the legislature was being used to wage class war. The rich did not have it all their own way though. Even in the eighteenth century, some MPs began to stand against this injustice, confident that they were reflecting the will of the people. They noted in Parliament the fact that in cases of theft juries, out of a natural aversion to condemning someone to their doom, would try and minimise the commercial value of the property that had been stolen in order to bring it below the capital penalty threshold. Others ridiculed laws that allowed the same punishment for patricide as there was for poaching; for treason as for destroying a hop bin; for associating with a gypsy as there was for killing the same gypsy. It was widely reviled that in many cases age was no barrier to execution. Boys as young as ten had received the death sentence, and 18 of 20 offenders would be aged under 21. There were, of course, opposing views. Some suggested that death itself was not in fact punishment enough, and that the level of suffering in the act of execution needed *increasing*. It was well known that Henry VIII would deliberately employ inexperienced executioners to kill those who had particularly offended him, resulting in multiple axe strikes being required to finish off the unfortunate victim, rather than the more accepted single blow. Frequently, passages from the Bible were quoted in support of each side of the argument, without any particular conclusion being reached. However, the pressure to modify the law grew incessantly, aided by the many distressing scenes that caused by the botched executions which resulted from a lack of a standardised manner of administering the ultimate penalty.

Originally, the executioner would be a town workman, such as a blacksmith, who engaged in the activity as a side-line; or would themselves be a criminal under the sentence, spared in order to undertake the unpopular task. Due to haphazard recruitment and a lack of training, there are recorded cases where convicted men and women were subjected to prolonged asphyxia only to survive for some time afterwards when finally cut down. 'Half Hanged' Smith dangled for two hours at Tyburn, before reviving, being pardoned, and entertaining crowds with tales of a tunnel of light, half glimpsed as he spun slowly in the breeze. Thomas Reynolds awoke in his coffin after being hung, only to succumb a short time later. William Duell awoke as the surgeons prepared to dissect his supposedly cold corpse. At the other extreme, some were horribly decapitated when the drop was miscalculated. Calcraft, one of several official Victorian executioners, was a notorious showman, usually drunk, a physical coward, who was often suspected of playing up to the crowds, deliberately guilty of half-hanging his victims and then swinging off their twitching bodies in order to finish the job. To much applause, it must be said. Such spectacles, coupled with the disparaging journalism of the likes of Dickens and Hardy, led to the ending of executions in public. Instead, the fatal act would take place inside the jail rather than on a gibbet in front of the walls. Hidden like a dirty secret, the death would be announced by raising a black flag and placing a solemn notice on the prison gates. Those against this move recited the need for the revenge upon the perpetrator to be seen, as a lesson and deterrent to others. The abolitionists on the other hand were generally in favour of attempts to reform the killer, stepwise or immediate, certain as they were that most murders were not the result of pre-meditated evil, but spur of the moment results of a temporary loss of humanity. Examination of the records of executions show a depressing predominance of alcohol induced temper rages amongst the poor resulting in unintended death, usually of an unfortunate woman by an inadequate and pathetic man. Slowly, the number of capital felonies were reduced; slowly pressure grew in Parliament to abolish, or modify, the death penalty. Unsuccessful attempts were made to segregate murder into different degrees of seriousness for many years, and much debate was expended on when any killing could be deemed as 'less serious' than another.

In the end, the country settled for the professionalization of the executioner's trade, and there grew to be dynasties of working-class men who developed the career as a family business. Names such as Billington, Pierrepoint, Allen and Marwood became synonymous with the grim trade. These men worked to make the process more humane and efficient by their dignified professionalism. They were not brutish sadists, but often quiet, thoughtful and feeling. By the twentieth century, the so called 'long drop' method of hanging had been developed to make the process more compassionate and effective, reducing suffering by its speed and instantaneous nature. As a result of careful planning, the neck would be broken at the level of the second cervical vertebrae, crushing and severing the spinal cord. A large degree of skill was required to do the job properly. The prisoner's height and weight were carefully measured, and in the days before the appointed time, the chief executioner and his assistant would watch the victim carefully, paying particular attention to the build, particularly that of the neck. These factors would govern how much rope was required to allow the falling body to generate the force necessary to break the spine cleanly. Out of sight, they would check the mechanism of the gallows, ensuring that there would be no glitches, making chalk marks where the condemned would stand, going through several dry runs before the big day. The prisoner would be in a special cell, guarded twenty-four hours by men who would prevent any attempt at suicide. It wouldn't do for the condemned to kill themselves before the state took its revenge. These guards would develop a sort of friendship with the walking dead, as they attempted to keep them entertained by reading, and playing chess, cards and other games. Chaplains would also attend, in case the intended victim wished to make their peace with God.

At appointed the hour, a secret door in the cell would swing open, and the intended would at last realise that there was no reprieve coming. Their arms would be swiftly pinioned, and they would be taken through the door, perhaps comforted by the intonations of the priest. They would stand on the chalk marks, and their legs would also be tied. Finally, a mask would be placed over the head, obscuring their view of the last faces they would ever see. The noose, a rope covered with leather, suspended through a metal eyelet, would be placed around the neck, the carefully constructed knot, the actual instrument of death, being positioned gently but firmly behind the ear.

There were no Hollywood-type last words or histrionics. There was no time, as the interval between the door swinging open and the trapdoor sliding apart was usually very short. In one case, it was recorded as only seven seconds. What would you do with the last seven seconds of your life, knowing that the last view you would have would be of the gallows and the inside of a hessian sack? Knowing that the '8 o'clock Walk' would be the last conscious act of your life? Would you despair, hope for salvation, rage against the dying of the light? Or go meekly to your end, knowing that it was deserved, and that a better place awaited you? Whether this speed actually did reduce suffering, we will never know. What is clear is that whilst some met their ends with dignity, others had to be drugged or dragged kicking and screaming to meet their Maker

There were also persistent fears that an innocent person could be subjected to an irreversible miscarriage of justice. It was estimated, for example, that over 40 wrongfully convicted persons were executed between 1802 and 1840, and it should be remembered that there was no appeal mechanism against a sentence or a jury's verdict until 1907. One famous case from the eighteenth century concerned innkeeper Jonathon Bradford, who was found standing over the dead body of a patron who had previously boasted about his wealth, covered in blood with a knife in his hand. Bradford always claimed his innocence, by the clichéd explanation so often now employed in detective fiction: roused by the sounds of someone in distress, he entered the room to find Mr Hayes dying, and had picked up the knife in confusion, only to be found in this manner by two witnesses who arrived soon after. The jury convicted him without even leaving the box, and he was executed in the traditional manner. However, 18 months later, the death bed confession of Hayes' footman, who had disappeared on the night of the murder, belatedly confirmed his own guilt and the innocence of Bradford. In 1876, William Hebron was convicted of the murder of PC Cock during a robbery. Being young, his sentence was commuted to penal servitude for life. The real murderer, the notorious Charles Peace, watched the trial to confirm that he was not a suspect. Finally arrested for another killing, the homicide of a Mr Dyson, the husband of a woman he was infatuated with, Peace made a confession to exonerate Hebron on the eve of his own execution. In 1885 John Lee, who was convicted of killing his landlady, became notorious as 'The Man they could not Hang' when, after being put through the ordeal of execution three times due to defective apparatus, he was reprieved. Released from jail in 1907, it was later suggested that this cruelly treated felon had, in fact, been innocent. As recently as 1935, Reginald Woolmington of Dorset, aged 21, had been sentenced to death for the shooting of his estranged 17-year-old wife with a shot gun, having taken the time to saw the barrel off first. Woolmington always claimed the shooting was accidental, that he intended to frighten poor Violet back to him by threatening suicide, but the gun had gone off in error. The Judge ruled that the evidence against him was so strong that the burden was on Woolmington to show his innocence. He was found guilty and sentenced to death. His appeal, on the grounds that the Judge misdirected the Jury, failed; but he was allowed to take his case to the House of Lords, where the conviction was quashed, on the grounds that the burden of proof should in fact remain on the prosecution to show guilt. This landmark judgement was widely taken to indicate by abolitionists that UK law had been mistakenly enacted by the judiciary in every capital case since 1762.

Slow but steady progress was therefore made as fewer and fewer murderers were committed to be hanged. Some killers' death sentences were commuted to life imprisonment, or they were detained at their Majesty's pleasure having been judged insane. As time progressed, fewer women were subject to execution, and the death penalty was eventually abolished for children. Apart from the war years, where there was a glut of spies and Irish rebels being disposed of, and if those shell shocked victims of martial law firing squads were excluded, the total number of executions in the twentieth century fell almost year on year, although there was still concern that those trapped in poverty, driven to drink, or killing their family out of misery, were disproportionately hastened to eternity by the state. A review of the crimes committed by those subject to the capital penalty are almost totally a string of sad, sorrowful domestic crimes committed by those in drink, who almost immediately took themselves to the police, made a confession and meekly accepted their fate.

Despite the general public support for hanging, there were still cases which caused widespread disturbance. In 1922, beautiful Edith Thompson was married to an older man. They couple took in a bright young fellow, Fred Bywaters, as a lodger, who became her lover. One day, Bywaters ambushed the couple whilst they were out walking, and killed the husband. Thompson, widely regarded by the papers as Bywater's *femme fatale* accomplice and the driving force behind the murder, was found guilty despite Bywater's assertion that he acted entirely of his own volition. Thompson unfortunately did not help herself at her trial, and the death sentence broke her mind. In the end, she earned the public sympathy that she was previously denied, when it was widely reported that she had to be carried screaming and almost insensible to her destiny. Such was the trauma of her distressing death, that it was believed to have contributed to the later suicide attempt of the executioner, Ellis. It was widely concluded that Thompson was executed for being an adulteress rather than an accomplice to murder. Tales such as this did more to advance the abolitionist cause in the public psyche than theoretical and philosophical arguments

In 1928, the Abolition of Capital Punishment Bill was introduced, an attempt to replace execution for murder with lifetime penal servitude. Many countries, it was argued, had abolished the death penalty without there being an increase in the number of murders. In addition, most murderers were not criminals until the point that they killed someone, and it was therefore uncertain how many murders the death penalty deterred. The Bill was unsuccessful, but the groundswell of pressure led to the creation of a Select Committee which reported in late 1930. The committee had been swathed in controversy, as the Chairman was reported to be biased, and six Conservative members had resigned from it in protest. It proposed a trial period of suspending the death penalty for five years. These recommendations were never implemented. Despite this, however, the number of executions of people under 21 fell, the overall number of executions reduced, and of the 17 women sentenced to death between 1923 and 1933, only one did not have her sentence commuted.

By the mid twentieth century, the abolition movement had grown into a significant political force, powered by strong personalities who did not care that the tide of media opinion, were against them. Right was on their side. *History* was on their side. The contempt that they were sometimes subjected to did not faze them. In many ways, they thrived on it. A typical example was the eccentric Violet van der Elst. Born in Middlesex 1882, to a coal porter and a washerwoman, she worked as a scullery maid before she married an older man. She invented the first brushless shaving cream and became a rich and respected businesswoman. After her first husband died, she then married the Belgian who gave her the memorable surname. They lived in an impressive home in Grantham that she purchased in her own right. She then dedicated her energies, and her fortune, to the abolitionist cause. A ferocious unstoppable force weighing in at an impressive 15 stone, she always wore black and was often to be found campaigning outside courts and prisons, particularly on the eve and mornings of executions, when she and her vocal supporters would loudly roar hymns as the dread hour approached. She herself was not above physically assaulting the executioner with her umbrella or getting her chauffer to drive her car directly through police cordons. A brass band would play the death march at the appointed time. Sometimes, planes would fly overhead, trailing black banners. Whether their efforts brought any kind of relief to the condemned cannot ever be known.

The abolitionist cause, then, had steadily grown over the centuries, gathering a head of steam that could not be ignored. In 1948, the abolitionists would score what they thought was to be a great victory, which was, to their despair, to turn out to be a spectacular own goal.

Chapter 6

The Honourable Gentleman

Houses of Parliament, Westminster
April 1948

After the Second World War the new, energised labour Government started to address the issue of capital punishment head on. By 1947, Chuter Ede, the Home Secretary, introduced a Criminal Justice Bill in an attempt to remove some of the more excessive punishments from the statute book. At this point, a back-bench MP who was a staunch abolitionist campaigner saw an opportunity to progress his cause and got himself appointed to the committee dealing with the Bill.

Silver-haired Samuel Silverman, known as Sydney, was MP for the Lancashire town of Colne which nestled on the Yorkshire Border near Burnley about seventeen miles from Blackburn. He was born into a poor Jewish draper's family in Liverpool in 1895 and won scholarships that enabled him to go to University and eventually became a solicitor. A life-long pacifist, during the First World War he had been a conscientious objector, suffering imprisonment for his beliefs. After a period lecturing at the University of Finland, he joined the Labour Party and eventually became an MP in 1935. He did a good job of representing the interests of his working-class constituency, but did not forget his pacifist beliefs, although they were challenged by the fervent anti-Semitism sponsored by the Nazis.

The surprise Labour victory after the War did not lead to high office, as he was too left wing for Prime Minister Atlee, and this suited him fine. Silverman was, according to colleagues vain, difficult, uncooperative, and self-righteous. He was fiercely independent and did not 'do' being a team player. A *New Statesman* article from 1956 described him as 'irritating', and 'cocky', with a pugilist's shoulders-back-chest-out stance, 'over occupied with his own shortness'. However, the main reason that he was irritating, conceded the journalist, was because he was generally proven to be correct. Passionate, pedantic, logical, forensic, courageous, he remained true to his beliefs, and voted independently on issues, a truly turbulent backbencher. A search of the British Pathé archive reveals a short clip of him making the case for abolition. Along with his colleagues, and against the wishes of Chuter Ede, he managed to add an amendment to the

Bill, proposing the total suspension of Capital Punishment for 5 years, as the 1930 Committee had previously recommended. Against the tide of traditional public opinion, they had support from such luminaries as George Bernard Shaw, who argued eloquently that the main failure of execution was that it removed any possibility of repentance and reform. Various other amendments to the Bill were proposed, but in the end Silverman's 5-year death penalty suspension was the one that remained.

On April 14th, 1948 the Criminal Justice Bill was debated in the House of Commons. The Government however faced a crisis. Chuter Ede felt that the Bill in this form was doomed, resulting in rejection of the whole package of reforms he had sponsored. It was clear that some members of the government would vote for gradual reform, but not the full abolition proposed. Rather than be responsible for the ruling party fracturing and not following an imposed Government position that was bound to fail, a free vote was allowed, except for the front bench who would all vote against. Ede was lambasted, having previously supported the case for abolition in 1938, but argued the Cabinet's view well. He outlined that the death penalty should be retained for some circumstances, and that there was no evidence that total abolition would not lead to a rise in violent crime. In support of his argument, he stated that in 1938, 97 murders had been committed; in 1946 it was 138, and in 1947 it was 134. Given that the number of violent assault convictions in these years was respectively 244, 370 and 402, he was convinced that the assaulters had been deterred from the final killing blow by the threat of death themselves. Others argued that it was not clear what would or could replace the death penalty, pointing out that the 10 to 15 years imprisonment forwarded instead was in fact shorter than that imposed for lesser crimes, such as manslaughter or armed robbery. Yet others referred to the fate of those individuals who were habitual killers, who made a trade of murder, such as Smith the notorious Brides in the Bath Murderer; and Neville Heath, the sexual sadist and killer, who, at his trial had pleaded casually 'Put me down as "not guilty", old boy'. Could such men ever be released? Was perpetual imprisonment the answer or even possible? Did they not *deserve* to be put down like mad dogs?

It was the Honourable Member for Wednesbury, Mr S Evans, who referred directly to the recent murder of Quinten Smith. He argued cogently that the majority of public opinion was not behind the blanket suspension of the death penalty. 'My Honourable Friend,' he declared, referring to the MP for Norwich, J Paton, who had argued strongly for abolition, 'said he spoke with fire in his belly when discussing this question.... but how truer it must be of the parents of that poor unfortunate child who was murdered in Lancashire last weekend!'

'Capital punishment did not save him!' interjected unidentified opposition.

But Evans had not finished. 'We must see these things in the correct perspective,' he persisted. Then he said the words that may have haunted Silverman in the months to come. 'Is it seriously suggested,' he asked, with chilling prescience, 'that someone who rapes a little girl and then kills her to destroy the evidence should be kept alive for *whatever* reason? I do not think so!'

Despite the confusion of the Government's official position, despite the strength of feeling and the determination of the opposition, the amendment was carried by 245 votes to 222. Silverman and his colleagues must have felt a sense of immense satisfaction that they had put the country on a higher moral path. They were sure, as the Bill headed off for further debate in the House of Lords, that they could smell success. For, from this point, the death penalty was suspended, and there would be no more judicial killings until the matter was settled.

It is not clear whether Silverman ever thought back to the sadly prophetic words of the MP for Wednesbury when the terrible events in Blackburn unfolded the following month; or, if he did, whether he had any premonition that his hubristic hopes of removing the death penalty forever were about to be destroyed for a generation by events that would occur almost literally in his own backyard.

Chapter 7

The Beast

Blackburn
May 14-15th 1948

Life was not progressing as promised in the Britain of 1948. In comparison to the war years, things were better, but really, we are just talking differing shades of grim. The new Labour Government struggled to improve many aspects of life by introducing wide-scale socialist experiments and innovations. The most important and urgent reform was the provision of healthcare, free at the point of delivery: a so-called National Health Service. Healthcare at this time was based on the ability to pay, local worker's insurance cooperatives, and charity. Those who could afford it could see a doctor when they wanted; get treated safely at home; or in a variety of private institutes.

The poor had no such option, unless part of a worker's health club. Town's General Hospitals were developed from workhouses, and Queen's Park in Blackburn was no different. It glowered over the town, a looming presence on a rocky ridge known as Whinney Heights, a remnant of that harsh and punishing form of charity preferred by the Victorians with their philosophy of the undeserving poor. Doctors had private practices to maintain their income and worked for the hospital either as a salaried intern, or for free. The hospitals themselves were funded by charities, local businesses, councils, and the rich. They had wards for planned admissions, but emergency care was catered for by so-called walking-in wards for casualties and the unwell. These opened at 9 am, and people who had reached the point of no return or suffered injuries attended to sit in the queue waiting to be seen. Those not lucky enough to have been consulted by closing time were sent home, to come back the next day, if they could. There was no formal dental care, and little formalised public health. For much of the late 19th Century the rivers running through Blackburn had been little more than open sewers, although the recognition that disease was spread by poor sanitation had begun to change this. However, although changes had been made, health reform remained haphazard and decentralised, and the province of enthusiasts, for decades.

It is hard from the comfort of the 21st Century to describe how different life was in the early to mid-twentieth. The first challenge for rich and poor alike was to actually survive being born. Today, maternal mortality in the first world runs at about 1 in 10000 pregnancies. In the early 1700s it was about 1 in 100, falling by the early 1900s to about 5- 7 women per 1000. In 1950's America it was recorded that up to 30% of infants died before the age of one. Whilst a substantial amount of these deaths were explained by poor nutrition and appalling social circumstances, disease was a major killer, spreading like wildfire due to the poor sanitation and slum housing. In 1948, parents and grandparents would recall the Spanish Flu pandemic of 1919, a disease that struck so swiftly that someone who was hale and hearty in the morning could be drowning on pus and blood by tea-time and in their shroud by supper. Even once that horror had passed, they could remember whole streets of children choking to death from diphtheria, hawking up chunks of lung tissue from whooping cough, succumbing to measles meningitis, or being left paralysed and wasted from polio. By 1948, some vaccinations existed, but were not in widespread use, and so the sporadic epidemics that harvested children by the score persisted.

Even if a child survived these risks, they could succumb to the chronic deterioration of TB, or die from blood poisoning from a minor wound, or slowly slip into multiple organ failure from smothering tonsillitis or develop heart failure from scarlet fever. Pneumonia, a severe chest infection, was particularly common. By 1948, the first trials with the antibiotic prototype streptomycin had begun, but for the overwhelming majority, the treatment of pneumonia remained entirely supportive.

Typically, the patient would develop a cough, dry and hacking, with a swinging temperature. They would become breathless, fatigued and soon they would be using all their energy just to breathe. Shortly afterwards, they would begin to expectorate large amounts of brown phlegm, described medically as *rusty sputum*, coloured so by the old blood that was mixed in with the infected mucus. Eventually, the patient would reach a crisis point. The temperature that would have inevitably been rising would either break, and they would settle, or they would continue to burn up, until they suddenly collapsed and died.

On 5th May, in 32 Princess Street, the heavily pregnant Emily Devaney and her husband Alfred, a foundry worker, watched in horror as young June Anne, aged 3 years 11 months, showed the classical signs. June was intelligent, with a wide vocabulary. Large for her years, she would easily pass for a child double her age, but before their eyes she began to fade away. In those days, the sick were kept at home if possible, but in June's case, it became impossible to manage with the other children in the house, the father's crushing hours of work, and her mother's impending labour.

June was admitted to the paediatric ward CH3 at the Queen's Park Hospital, where, over the next week, she made steady progress. She did so well, that she was due to be discharged home on the 14th May. However, Emily was threatening to go into labour, and the hospital was persuaded to keep June for one more night.

It is on such small decisions that destinies are made and broken. Had the hospital staff not taken pity on the Devaneys and discharged June on the 14th as planned she perhaps would have lived a full and fruitful life. She would have gone to school, got a job in a shop or a factory; or perhaps she would have remembered the kindness of the nurses and the crispness of their uniforms and gone into caring herself. She might have broken hearts, and had her own broken; she would have been a teenager in the fifties and sixties, been a fan of Cliff Richard and Tommy Steele; or had arguments with her friends about whether she should snog John, Paul, George or Ringo; met a boy, got married; had children, grandchildren; or lived a spinster; died at a ripe old age, or prematurely in an accident; moved abroad as a *ten pound Pom*, or lived her whole life in the one, small dreary part of a tiny, amazing and industrious island. But it was not to be.

In the last minutes of the 14th May, a lone cab pulled up outside of Queen's Park, one of Blackburn's many formal gardens laid out for the benefit of the townsfolk by the mill owners. It lay at the base of the hill that the hospital stood on, in the nearby district of Audley Range. After a short pause, a figure stepped out of the taxi into the shaded, tree lined street at the corner of the Park and the nearby quarry land known colloquially as *the Shorrock Delph*. There was no marked entrance to the works, no railings; merely two wooden stumps secured by a low, loose chain. No barrier to anyone, certainly not a determined man. The car drove off, and after a pause, the figure trotted towards the hill.

Today, there is a school on what was once the Delph, but the pathway that winds up from Queen's Park to the Hospital remains. The path is still used by park workers, joggers and walkers and is shaded with a variety of trees, shrubs and flowers. In the summer, it can be quite beautiful. The path slopes upwards to the Heights, and it is quite a climb to reach the thick stone wall that marks the boundary of the hospital grounds, hard to get to the top without being short of breath. In 1948, the wall ran around most, but not all, of the hospital's boundary, curving around the back of ward CH3, turning along the edge of the abrupt drop to the Delph. The wall then ended, having collapsed at the north west corner and was replaced with a slatted, picket fence of chestnut wood entangled with barbed wire. It is not clear how old the fence, and therefore the breach in the wall, was, but the fence was in a state of poor repair and had been for God knew how long. It was a dark night, but the figure made his way confidently upwards without injury. Without stumbling, he located a gap where the rickety fence had also collapsed, leaving a space big enough for a man to pass through. After hoisting himself up, the figure might have paused to take his breath.

Today, he would be standing in a car park, gravelled and tarmacked. In 1948, it was a vast grass prairie. With his back to the town, far below, he would have looked across the lawn at the Victorian facade of the Hospital, with its grand entrance and two wings. Today, this is offices, but then it contained the lying-in wards, the maternity suite and operating theatres. To his right, he would have seen the road that led to the Porter's Cabin at the main entrance off Haslingden Road. Looking left, he would have seen the Nursing Home, opened in 1926, now Union Offices and storage. To the left of that, stood the wooden L-shaped children's wards, CH3, on its own, isolated from the main buildings. The figure walked from the fence towards the solitary ward, standing outside the veranda, watching and listening. The big brass porch doorknob glistened dully in the partial moonlight, sullenly illuminating the lopsided ward sign with the faded number 3, white on a black background. Flat roof, faded paintwork, cracked windows loose in their frames. He could clearly hear the sounds of a nurse humming and clattering around in the kitchen area, carried to him on the breeze. So clear was the sound through the thin walls, he could probably visualise her every move, note her every location as she went about her duties.

As he listened, the figure slowly took off his shoes, put them carefully on the veranda, and waited. And waited. And waited.

Chapter 8

Little Girl Lost

Ward CH3, Queen's Park Hospital
May 14th-15th 1948

At night, one nurse looked after both of the wards within the CH3 building. The pre-fab consisted of two wings, joined through a pivotal corridor, with the kitchen area in the middle. One wing was referred to as the 'Baby's Ward' where the children slept in cots. It was this ward where June Ann Devaney dreamt her last dreams. The 'Toddler's Ward' held the older children, who slept soundly in beds. The nurse's duties were to maintain observations on the patients, comfort and treat them when necessary, and make ready for the morning workload.

The Cottontown Killer

Nurse Gwendoline Humphreys had come on duty at 11:30pm, took the handover from the outgoing staff, did her initial rounds and began to make preparations in the kitchen for the morning breakfast. As usual, porridge was on the menu, and Nurse Humphreys began to clean the utensils she would need. She was interrupted by a cry from the Baby's Ward. When she went in, she found that young Michael Tattersall, in the cot next to June Anne, was fretful. The nurse glanced briefly at June as she comforted him. He settled quickly and she was able to return to the kitchen at about twenty past midnight. Everything seemed in order.

A short time later, she thought she heard a child's cry from the vicinity of the porch. She went to the door and looked for some time out into the night. Again, she saw nothing untoward, so she checked on the children in the ward, and returned to the kitchen. It was a real concern that one of the children might sleepwalk out into the 70 acres of the hospital grounds because the main door did not lock. No doubt the Public Assistance Board and the Board of Hospital Guardians had this on their list of repairs along with the fence, but let us be charitable and say that, fully occupied as they would have been with the impending transfer of the hospital to the management of the new fledgling National Health Service in July, they had inadvertently allowed it to slip down their list of priorities. It would be harsh indeed to think that they risked the security of the children to save a few pennies in straightened times. As she returned to the kitchen, Nurse Humphreys passed a trolley which had three large, chunky Winchester bottles on it, each of which held about two litres of distilled water, used to make up medicines, wash wounds and keep dressings clean. In the kitchen, she was slicing bread before she got interrupted again, this time by a child from the Toddler's Ward. She found the crying girl, took her to the kitchen, fed her bread and jam, and gave her a warm drink. It was about half midnight at this point, and it took her about fifteen minutes to settle the girl and return her to bed.

It is presumed that she did not feel a chill during these activities as the porch door was opened and silently closed.

The mysterious figure had finally broken his paralysis, and at some point, had padded lightly into the ward. He wandered purposefully up past the cots, keeping his ears open so that he could track the nurse by the sound of her movements. He hid in the empty end rooms, with their bay windows when he thought she was near, and then returned when he judged it safe, pausing briefly to stare at the sleeping occupants of the cots against the west wall of the ward. The last cot contained June Anne, and he must have stared down at her for a short time, whilst terrible thoughts burned through his head.

Eventually, he bent over, and picked her up, banging Michael Tattersall's cot and disturbing him slightly. He lifted June Anne, who wriggled drowsily, and like any young child, aware that an adult was moving them, and feeling safe, and comforted, she nestled her head on his shoulder, and looped an arm around his neck. Then, without a backward glance, the figure walked through the door, and stepped out into the cool of the night with her.

Nurse Humphreys settled the young girl back into the Toddler's Ward and returned to the Baby Ward. She immediately noticed something was wrong. She must have registered several things at once: one of the Winchester bottles on the floor under the end cot, the open porch door letting in the frigid night air, a set of what looked like bare footprints showing that someone had walked up and down the ward, an open window in the bayed area. The horribly empty cot. Dear God, the cot.

After a brief search, she alerted her superiors, and they began a proper trawl of the area. By this time, though, it was already too late. June Anne had already been murdered.

Whilst the hue and cry began, and whilst the level of activity grew, the figure calmly walked back to the ward to retrieve his shoes, and then retraced his steps back to the wall. With barely a glance at the dead child, he went back through the fence, down through the Delph, across the dark streets, and was back at his house by about 1 am. He took off his suit, hanging it carefully; put on his battle dress which was his only other clothes; and bedded down on the sofa for the rest of the night. It is possible that his sleep was dreamless. If there was any justice, it was not.

James Watts & Thomas Watts

Blackburn, Lancashire
May – August 1948

Chapter 9

Alarm

It is hard for those of us who live in the age of instant pan-global communication, internet, *Facebook*, *Twitter*, *Snapchat* and *Instagram* to understand how slowly calls for help could be communicated until very recently. Dedicated telephone lines to police stations were only fully implemented nationally after the callous murder of PC Gutteridge because of the serious delays from the discovery of his body to the time that police were finally called to attend. A dedicated general emergency telephone number system-999- was rolled out in London in 1937 following a fire in Wimpole Street two years earlier in which 5 women died. Astonishingly, a neighbour had tried phoning to raise the alarm with the Fire Service but had effectively been placed on 'hold' by the Welbeck Telephone Exchange. Some frustrations never change.

The 999 scheme was rolled out to all major cities after World War II, and only to the whole UK in 1976 when the telephone system became fully automated. Before the regular police use of phones, news could only travel as fast as a man on a horse or a vehicle, or through the telegraph system. Telephones were not in widespread use, commonly confined to the rich and officialdom. National and global messages were sent to the public via the one-way medium of radio. Communication was something that was given to the majority by the minority.

By the standards of the time, the speed at which the alarm was raised after June was noticed to be missing was astonishingly fast, because the stakes were so high. The manhunt was well underway by the time that the local newspapers got wind of the tragedy. Of course, the forces of law and order were unable to stop the spread of any gossip, and so the whole town was aware of the murder before the first editions were published. By then, the police were already in possession of all the information that would eventually identify the killer, except his name and address.

The timescale of events of the fatal night is clearly defined.

June Anne Devaney was missed from the ward at about 01:20 on the morning of 15th May 1948. At 01:55, Blackburn Borough Police received a frantic phone call from the Queen's Park Hospital following a brief search which had failed to find her. Local police rapidly attended the scene and by 03:17 her body was found, a short distance of 283 feet from the door of the Children's Ward, by PC Edward

Parsons. The scene was later covered by a white sheet, which for days flapped limply in the wind, clearly visible from the town, a constant, horrible reminder; a monstrous semaphore signalling to the surrounding area the terrible events that had occurred. At 4am, Chief Constable Looms attended with the police surgeon Dr Gilbert Bailey. They were accompanied by Detective Sergeant Woodmansey of the Lancashire Constabulary.

Looms realised almost immediately that the resources required to deal with the murder and the resultant public disorder that might result if a swift and successful conclusion was not reached were beyond his means, and it is now that his organisational skills and deep knowledge of the job of policing came to the fore. It is possible that his experiences in 1935, as well as his recent involvement in the Quinten Smith murder enquiry, were driving his thinking. Looms later described the murder as both 'bestial' and 'brutal' and obviously did not want to take any chances that might impair the ability to apprehend the culprit. Within five minutes of being informed of the terrible crime, he had contacted his opposite number, Sir Archibald Horden, the Chief Constable of the Lancashire Constabulary, who agreed to place his facilities at Looms' full disposal. Soon, Assistant Chief Constable Thornton of the Lancashire Force arrived with the radio cars that would enable them to better coordinate the search for clues and the perpetrator. The Forensic Officers, under the command of D.C.I. Campbell of the Fingerprint Bureau, were contacted by Horden, and arrived on the scene by 05:10. In addition, Looms wasted no time in contacting Scotland Yard. There was the distinct possibility that the murder could be linked with the events in Farnworth, and Looms knew that they would have an interest in a similar case that had occurred only twenty short miles away. It was this call that catapulted Capstick and Stoneman back on their way to Blackburn.

Chapter 10

Crime Scene

As a workhouse, Queen's Park Hospital had been deliberately built in a prominent position so that it could be seen from all over the district, to strike terror into the hearts of those lax enough to crash-dive into poverty. Now, it was a beacon of fear for a completely different reason.

The layout of the hospital at that time is very clear from contemporary aerial photographs. It sat on the crest of a ridge to the South East of Blackburn. To the east were farms, and Shadsworth Hall. To the south, the roads to Haslingden and Darwen. The frontage of the hospital was about a quarter of a mile, but the only official entry was from Haslingden Road, opposite *the Observatory* public house past the Porter's Lodge where all visitors had to report and 'sign in'. The hospital site has grown vastly in recent decades, and the original location of some departments can only be identified by the remnants of once grand buildings that are now classrooms, libraries and administration

The 1948 site was bounded to the south by Old Bank Lane, a road which mainly no longer exists, having been mostly subsumed into the hospital grounds; the nurses' home abutted onto this thoroughfare. To the north it was bordered by a 60-foot drop, which stretched down towards the eponymous Queen's Park with its bowling greens and boating lake. Further away to the North East lay the district of Audley, and its reservoir. The Delph merged with both Queens' Park, and, to the North West, Grimshaw Park, which is now an industrial estate. These relatively green areas blended into the industrial districts serviced by the Leeds and Liverpool Canal, which unloaded locally at the industrial area at Eanam Wharf. This northern boundary of the hospital grounds was secured by the old wall, the northwest corner of which was the section nearest the children's ward

This wall was often covertly scaled by young Romeos seeking out their nursing sweethearts. The son of a contemporary police officer remembered his father moaning about the fact that, despite the terrible murder, young men continued to engage in this activity during the investigation, and were often apprehended, and sent on their way with a telling off and an official warning.

It was by this wall that June's body lay.

The Children's ward-CH3- sat at the rear of the main buildings, between the Nurses' Home and the wall. The baby ward section contained 12 cots, and on 15th May, June had been the oldest resident. CH3 was the furthest ward from the Porter's Lodge and was, therefore, fatally vulnerable. However, this also made it easy to secure for the forensic teams to do their vital work. Including staff and patients, the average population of the hospital was estimated to be about 1200 people at any one time. It would be a formidable task to exclude these as suspects.

Chapter 11

Taskforce

The first job for the police was to secure the hospital premises. One team was assigned to create a perimeter, whilst the ward itself was isolated until the forensic team from Police Headquarters at nearby Hutton could arrive.

A Hospital Investigation Taskforce was immediately established under the command of Detective Chief Inspector McCartney whose job was to ensure that every male member of hospital staff, and every male who had visited the hospital, whether relatives or merely tradesmen, were identified, interviewed and fingerprinted. It seems that the people who were contacted were so stunned by the horror that had visited the hospital that they submitted to fingerprinting without protest. In a haunting reflection of the nineteenth century hunt for the child-killer Fish, local bloodhounds were brought in to assist in the search for clues. Sadly, they succeeded only in identifying a trail from the Children's Ward to the site where June's body was found.

After June was discovered, PC Parkinson along with Inspector William Wilson had gone to Princess Street to rouse Albert Devaney from his bed to tell him his daughter was missing. Albert, sensitive to his wife's feelings, had told her only that several locals were being deputised to search for a missing child. He was taken to June's body, to find her face -down in the grass, feet towards the distant CH3 ward. Her nightgown was raised, and it was obvious she had, in the terminology of the day, been 'interfered with'. A human bite mark was horribly visible on her buttock. She was covered in blood, and it was clear that her head had been dashed repeatedly with force against the wall, by someone who had swung her by the ankles.

Naturally Albert was inconsolable. Worse, he had the knowledge that his poor, dead daughter would have to stay on the cold wet grass until the crime scene had been thoroughly documented. So distraught was Albert that he had to enlist the help of a neighbour to tell his spouse. There is, of course, no easy way to deliver such devastating news, and Mrs Devaney was understandably hysterical.

Police Photographer Sgt H.B. Taylor took photos of the child *in situ* and she lay by the wall under an improvised cover until Capstick and Stoneman arrived. Capstick was a hard man, but he admitted in his autobiography that he saw the young corpse through a 'mist of tears'. He wrote 'I swore, standing there in the rain, that I would bring her murderer to justice if I had to devote the rest of my life to the search. I would find him if he hid himself in the bowels of Hell.'

Melodrama aside, Capstick was a determined and pragmatic man. He knew his reputation, and that of the local force, and the Yard, was on the line, and that he needed to formulate a strategy to resolve this case, and soon. Even so, his wife's words must still have echoed around his head. *Find him, Jack. Whatever it takes.*

At last, June was taken to rest at the mortuary where the post mortem examination confirmed that she had suffered terrible injuries. Swabs and blood samples were carefully collected from her remains, and stored as evidence by Noel Jones, the staff biologist. Hair and fibres from the bloodstained grass and the fatal wall, scrapings from her fingernails and clothing, were all filed and documented. It was soon determined that June was blood group A, a finding that would be important later on. Having finished at the crime scene, Capstick and Stoneman attended the post mortem, and then travelled directly to Blackburn Police HQ on Northgate. They were met personally by Looms who pledged his entire support for Capstick's investigation. This was no time for personal pride or petty turf battles. One of their own, a 'Blackburn Baby', had been taken and defiled. Looms was keen that the case was closed quickly and was more than happy for control of the investigation to pass to Capstick. Capstick's first major decision was to order the dapper Inspector Bill Barton, a born organizer, to search every 'boarding house, pub, hotel and doss house' in the town, to check every train station, every factory, every vagrant, every stranger. From the state of the body, the villain would have been covered in blood, and he advised that every laundry, dry cleaner's, tailors and dyers was investigated.

In the meantime, Capstick appraised the Yard of the importance of acting fast, and by the evening, he had been reinforced by other officers from the Met including Inspector Wilf Daws and Sergeant Ernie Mullen. Eventually, Capstick would have his team further supplemented by another officer, Inspector Norman. Once they arrived, he and Stoneman were able to eat, sleep and shave.

All this activity. All this fear, and panic, and politics and bureaucracy. It is easy to see how the investigation could have turned into a shambles, with three different forces stumbling over each other, allowing crime scenes to be contaminated, and destroyed, vital clues to be lost, large areas of possible investigation to be missed. However, both Looms and Capstick, different as they were, were too professional and organised to let that happen. Capstick was already confident that the net was inevitably tightening, even at this early stage. However, he was not a patient man, being a great believer that action was better than inaction, and that hunches were a legitimate adjunct to the science of police-work. Early experience had taught him that there was no substitution for feet on the ground, and thoroughness. Attacking an investigation *en masse*, head-on, with a highly visible police presence, would not only increase the likelihood of success, but would put pressure on the perpetrator, who was then more likely to make a mistake and reveal himself. This was a case where brute force would do better than a *softly, softly catchee monkey* approach. Capstick had already made a good, firm start, and he already felt that it was only a matter of time before he had his man.

It is not clear at what stage he realised that radical action would require to be taken. Perhaps the idea to adapt the lessons learnt from his previous experiences was already germinating, waiting for the right trigger to make it bloom.

Chapter 12

Forensics

D I Campbell had Ward CH3 so thoroughly mapped that even now, over seventy years later, we can be absolutely certain of its lay-out and construction. The ward was a brick and pre-fab building which had been meant to house the sick children of the borough temporarily until a more permanent structure was built. As is the way of these things, despite its wholly unsuitable and constantly deteriorating condition, the ward was not finally demolished until 1983, after local MP Jack Straw raised the matter of long delayed local hospital improvements in Parliament. It is astonishing to think that for over three decades the people of Blackburn had to allow their children to be treated in a ward from which a local child had been kidnapped and horribly murdered. Someone somewhere must have decided that such sentiments were of low consequence when determining the funding of hospital modernisation priorities. Hopefully, they had just been thoughtless, rather than an apparatchik who had made a specific decision that respect for people and their sensibilities weighed little when it came to pounds, shillings and pence.

The main door to the ward opened from a west-facing veranda into a short corridor, and was operated by the distinctive brass doorknob with its fatal, faulty mechanism. To the right was the entrance to the Toddler's Ward and the Sister's Office. Opposite was the kitchen area, the linen cupboard and the bathroom. To the left, was the door to the Baby Ward. The ward contained a dozen cots, arranged against both walls. June had been in the cot that was third on the left-hand side, if you stood with your back to the ward entrance. There were four windows, and two other doors in this wall. Looking in through these windows, he could see a table at which the children ate and played and the footprints, made by stockinged feet, which traversed the ward, stopping ominously by the dead child's cot.

At the top of the ward were a medicine cabinet on which the three large Winchester bottles were normally kept, and a wheeled mobile examination screen. At the end of the ward was a door that led to three toilets on the left and an office area on the right with three further windows. The external exit from this annex was locked.

It was a large and complex area to analyse, but Campbell was a methodical man, who did not jump to conclusions or act in haste. An acknowledged expert in his field, he later became renowned for inventing the first non-toxic finger print dye, *lanconide*.

Having been given an outline of events by Looms, Campbell toured the outside of the building as the sun rose, looking for signs of any forcible entry. He soon deduced that they would find none, as there were six unlocked doors and open windows in the annex in the north end of the building, and, as noted, the main door did not fasten at all. Every external surface which might retain a fingerprint was dusted using the standard squirrel hairbrush coated with *hydrerg-cum-creta*, and the results photographed with a Graflex camera using orthochromatic film. The resulting fingerprints were analysed, documented, and compared.

Having traversed the external perimeter, he then moved inside the ward area itself, noting its layout. He drew chalk lines around the footprints, already trying to determine how useful information could be lifted from them. He also realised that the large Winchester bottle that lay under the dead girl's cot had been deliberately moved from its fellows at the end of the ward. The staff denied doing so, and therefore this was an item that had probably been handled by the killer. This bottle and the fingerprints that it retained would be vital to the investigation. Each revealed impression was labelled photographed, and catalogued.

The bottle of course held the prints of anyone who had ever touched it. Fortunately, the fresher prints would always be bigger than the older ones, but even so, Campbell would need a collection of staff fingerprints to eliminate those that were not pertinent.

By the end of the day, Campbell had isolated 8 prints of interest from the bottle. They were remnants of a right middle and right ring finger, three fragments, and most importantly, clear prints of a left thumb, ring, middle and forefinger, and a palm print. It seemed that the bottle had been handled twice by the intruder; once by the neck, as if it could be used as a weapon. Had the nurse returned to the ward from the kitchen area at the wrong moment, it looked like would have ended badly for her.

Campbell started his investigation at the north end of the ward, sweeping from the open windows down towards the west side, where the girl's cot had lain.

He identified the same fingerprints on the second, third and fourth cots, and on the north and south facing doors as were on the bottle. Having tried powder on the footprints, without success, he photographed them utilising a method which clarified the detail they contained. No-one legitimately on the ward had walked around in stocking feet and so these, then, were traces left directly by the killer. Each was carefully measured with a ruler.

Campbell now had a formidable store of evidence at his disposal: fingerprints; foot prints; blood and hair taken from the body, including a pubic hair and swabs; red and blue fibres that had been left by the socks that made the footprints embedded in the wax floor; and samples of the child's own tissues. He and his colleagues set to work interpreting the information. Capstick sought him out, and Campbell discussed all the evidence with him, particularly highlighting the importance of the fingerprints. It was clear that the prints would be the key to the case, and it was this that would inspire Capstick to formulate his subsequent bold plan.

Chapter 13

Lockdown

Capstick already knew many of the officers at Blackburn from the Farnworth investigation, and he regarded Bob McCartney as resourceful, and methodical. McCartney always kept his pockets full of pens, pencils and notepaper, and he had just the sort of job the shortest man on the Blackburn Force excelled at. In the first few days, Capstick charged McCartney with an initial exercise to fingerprint all the hospital staff, and the residents of the nearest streets.

McCartney and the hand-picked eleven men on his team acted swiftly. They knew that they had to isolate the hospital to preserve the crime scene, and that the longer they took to eliminate staff from enquiries the further away the killer might get; and so, McCartney's taskforce took several steps simultaneously. One group trawled the staffing, visitors and tradesmen's records, going back over two years, to identify anyone who possibly may have left their trace on the ward. Staff were then methodically detained, and fingerprinted. Their prints were then sent to Hutton to be compared with those of over 125,000 known felons.

By 4pm on the 15th, the hospital had been, in Capstick's words, 'frozen', isolated and locked down. No one was allowed in, and no one was allowed out without having their dabs taken. By 6pm, it became clear that this line of enquiry was, as expected, fruitless.

By the 19th May, they had fingerprinted another 642 individuals who had access to the ward in the previous 24 months and been able to discount them all as suspects. This was a great achievement in itself, but what was to come would eclipse it.

Chapter 14

Charley Artful

B y the 18th May, thanks to Campbell, the Police were able to hold their first co-ordinated briefing session at Northgate. During this meeting, the investigators were able to review their evidence and update their provisional timeline considerably

The Hospital had rung the station on the evening of the 14th to report a Peeping Tom. A figure had been seen lingering around the bushes, and when challenged by two nurses replied 'Hush! Don't tell anyone.' He insisted on escorting them like a gentleman to the Nurses' Home, but they later saw him with his face pressed up against a window. Any other day, this might have been attributed to a nurse's misplaced sweetheart, waiting for the end of shift so as to have a tryst with his beloved. However, this man, of whom only a vague description would exist, now became a significant figure of interest. The two nurses in question were later unsuccessfully driven around the town in an attempt to identify the voyeur from random passers-by. Capstick would eventually locate him, visiting his wife who was a hospital inpatient. The shamefaced individual was eliminated from the enquiry, and given a stern talking to.

Another distraction was the glut of false confessions that the police had to deal with. Godwin in his account of the later trial gives an account of one persistent such individual, a 'young lad'. This youth confessed not only to the murder of June Devaney, but had also previously claimed responsibility for the death of Quinten Smith. In a macabre twist of fate, the same youth killed his younger brother in July 1948. Godwin does not name the culprit, but from his description it was probably 16-year-old Kenneth Lester, of Cheetham Hill Manchester who was found unfit to stand trial, and so was detained indefinitely in an asylum. Lester died in the 1970's.

The witnesses had confirmed that the last time that the fingerprinted bottle was seen to be in its proper place was about 00:15, and that June was known to be definitely in her cot was 00:20 on the 15th.

Nurse Humphreys was off the ward at 00:40, but returned when she thought she heard a girl's voice. There was nothing amiss as far as she could tell at this time. She was then distracted to the Toddler ward. She returned at 01:20, and, on feeling a draft, noticed that the door was now open. Returning to the ward, she then realised that June was missing, possibly having failed to notice it before because the cot side had remained up. The bottle was now seen to be under the cot. Nurse Humphreys completed a preliminary search, and by 01:30 had rung for help from the night sister. A further search revealed no trace of the girl, and the hospital management were informed. The police were called at 01:55, and June's remains were discovered at 03:17. There was therefore only a narrow window of about 60 minutes when the intruder could have entered the ward, and only a period of 40 minutes, between 00:40 and 01:20 when June could have been taken.

The meeting also considered the information that they had gathered about the killer from the evidence. Everyone was surprised by the level of detail that Campbell could give them.

Firstly, although it may have been a seemingly obvious fact, it was clear from the evidence that they were dealing with only one man. Secondly, the killer had definitely gained access to the hospital grounds through the broken fence. As the path up to the fence through the Delph was obscure, and the killer was able to negotiate this in the dark, it was felt that the culprit was almost certainly a local, or at least had a large degree of local knowledge. He appeared to have headed straight for the children's ward, and so he knew where it was. If he was indeed local, it may have been that he knew one of the patients there.

By a process of elimination, Campbell was very confident that the freshest prints on the bottle were in fact those of the killer. Sadly, these prints did not match any on the existing criminal database, and so could not be traced to any known local current felon. However, the nature of the fingerprints gave further important details about the culprit. The spread of the palm and the prints on the bottle was large, so they were almost definitely male, and gave an indication of build. A lack of scarring, coarseness and wear on the ridges and whorls showed that the owner was not a manual labourer and indicated a degree of youth.

The footprints showed that he had entered the ward through the north door, and circumnavigated it at least once, pausing by a window where several fibres were found. The footprints revealed not only the size of his feet, 10 ¼, but the length of his stride, and thereby an estimated height of about 5'10". This tied in with the fact that June had been lifted from the cot without dropping the side, indicating a tall person had abducted her. This information effectively eliminated the ward porter from consideration, as he was only 5 feet four inches, with tiny feet. The footprints had yielded errant blue and red threads from the socks that the killer had worn as he had stalked the ward.

Local. Male. 5'10". Size 10 ¼ feet. Blue socks, with a red thread. Young. Not a manual labourer. Possibly known to one of the patients.

Everyone in this meeting knew that they were tantalisingly close to identifying their man. They could almost visualise his silhouette, sketched out by Campbell, almost see him in the shadows. But he remained a shape, without detail, without features

They had all the clues they needed to identify him when they found him, now they needed to close the net, and quickly. It was time for decisive action.

It was at this point that Capstick expanded upon his previous idea of fingerprinting all of those who lived near the hospital; a notion that had been fermenting for some days, audacious and pragmatic, and typical of the man.

'There's only one way to get our man,' he announced to the room. 'We are going to fingerprint every male in Blackburn and district between the ages of 14 and 90. Every male, no matter how unlikely, who is not actually bedridden.'

There must have been a gasp of amazement as the enormity of the order became apparent. There were over 30,000 homes in Blackburn, approximately 120,000 people. The demographic that Capstick described must contain over 40,000! Looms himself pointed out that the public might not co-operate, and the task itself might take months. This is where the force of Capstick's formidable personality played a key role. 'Those fingerprints are something our man will never lose, even after he's dead. He can't escape from them,' he reasoned. 'As for co-operation, I don't believe there is a decent man, or woman, in Blackburn who would not go with us 100%.'

Looms must have been astounded by the scale, the audacity, of the idea. The logic was however simple and inescapable. Anyone who declined to co-operate at all would immediately become a suspect, as would all suicides and attempted suicides until their fingerprints eliminated them. Anyone who absconded from the area would also immediately come under suspicion, and be made subject of an all-points bulletin manhunt, until they were returned for printing. In addition, local hospitals would be asked to report anyone who attended with a finger injury, in case they had attempted to destroy their tell-tale guilt.

Up until this point, the main advantage the killer had was that he was able to hide himself amongst the population of his hometown. Capstick's plan, if implemented, turned this advantage on its head, transforming Blackburn from a safe haven into a trap from which there could be no escape. The killer could hide, but he literally could not run.

Capstick also discussed his plan to ensure that the town would cooperate. He would start the process by personally asking the Mayor of Blackburn, and his council, to be the first to provide prints

No minutes exist of the meeting that Looms and Capstick had with the Mayor, Alderman Sugden, and the Councillors. It can be imagined how they initially reacted, but once again the bluff unstoppable force that was Capstick overcame all obstacles.

Looms had to give an undertaking that after the investigation, all the prints would be destroyed and that during the exercise that they would not be used for any other investigation, but Capstick must have left the meeting in a buoyant mood. The Council had all agreed and donated their prints and encouraged the public to do the same. He would get his man. He knew it. It was inevitable. The trap was sprung. Time, which had been against them, was now firmly on their side.

Nothing could go wrong.

Chapter 15

Painting the Town Black

The mammoth task of printing virtually every male in the town was again delegated to the arch-organiser Bill Barton. He devised a systematic and detailed process to ensure that all relevant residents were identified and located. He and his team trawled the electoral roll to identify those households containing males of the right demographic in the town's 14 voting wards, each of which was further sub-divided into 3 or 5 sectors. By 23rd May the information required had been gathered from the registers, and the task could begin.

Barton had a team of about 20 officers. Taking each district one at a time, and starting with the hospital and Northgate as centres, the officers called at every house in turn. Carrying all the necessary equipment with them, inkpads and 3 $^3/_8$ inch cards, the fingerprint team would arrive at the selected home, identify the appropriate males, gently roll their fingers on the ink, and then on the card, and get the individual to countersign them. They then repeated the process at every household, from 8am till 10pm every day, including weekends. Slowly, surely, they made their way around the town, its terraces, its mansions, its villas, its byways and highways, its backstreets, cul-de-sacs, farmhouses and shanties. Every evening, the cards would be handed in to the night officer, and forwarded on to the lab at Hutton, where Campbell and his team would work diligently throughout the night, and the next day, building a database, compiling, cataloguing, comparing, excluding.

Soon, the district was filled with larger and larger numbers of men and boys with the tell-tale blackening of their fingers, leaving smudges on their shirts, their work-tools, their wage packets and newspapers. It was as if the spreading stain of dark suspicion was slowly engulfing the town

It was a very public campaign, which for the moment had full support. If his gambit failed, Capstick would suffer a very obvious fall from grace, and could take Looms, and possibly the reputation of Scotland Yard, with him. The fingerprint campaign made not only the local papers, but the nationals and internationals. It would have been hard to keep the matter secret, but Capstick had actively publicised the campaign, wanting the killer to feel the net inexorably tightening, to feel to his core that justice was coming. However, days turned into weeks, and every lack of a positive match brought new disappointment, and the risk of humiliating failure grew.

As a result, it was also decided that in addition to the local population, there would be fingerprints taken from the 3,600 patients who had been recently discharged from mental health institutions throughout the north of England, particularly if they had a history of indecency. All persons with recent diagnosis of venereal disease, or a diagnosis of schizophrenia or epilepsy, or those guilty of 'committing acts contrary to nature' (that is, homosexuals) were all to be considered worthy of helping the police with their enquiries. There were also approximately 13,000 persons of unknown nationality within a 20-mile radius of Blackburn, such as members of the Free Polish Army, or German POWs, and displaced refugees, so the enquiries were widened into this area of interest. Every 'casual' or vagrant in the area was also to be rounded up and questioned.

If the killer was relatively young, he could have been or still might be serving military personnel. Had he been stationed abroad, it was possible he may have committed a similar crime, unknown to UK officials. So, as copies of the fingerprints were being sent out nationally anyway, it was decided to also send them to British military authorities overseas, along with a request for them to check their records for any active personnel or reservists with a history of such offences. By 15th June, letters would have been sent to the four corners of the British Empire, from Australia, to Canada, from Belize to Singapore, from Hong Kong to India. The accompanying letter read:

Dear Sir
MURDER OF JUNE ANN DEVANEY AT
BLACKBURN ON
15th MAY 1948

The Cottontown Killer

During the early hours of 15th May 1948, the Children's Ward at Queen's Park Hospital, Blackburn was entered and June Ann Devaney, 3 ½ years old, was taken from her cot. She was later found murdered in the hospital grounds, having been the victim of a sexual assault.

Before taking the child from her cot, the culprit carried a Winchester bottle from a trolley at the end of the ward and left it beside the cot from which the child was taken

The bottle has several digital impressions which, up to the present, have not been identified. Below are illustrated two of the impressions disclosed on the bottle and I have to ask if you will be so good as to cause them to be compared with the fingerprints in your collection with a view to establishing the identity of the offender in this case

The impression "A" which is one of a sequence was made by a left forefinger; the left middle finger of the same hand is an ulnar loop with at least 15 ridge counts, and the left ring finger is an ulnar loop with at least 11 ridge counts. The tip only of the left little finger appears.

The impression "B" was made by a left thumb, and it is probable, but not certain, it was made by the same hand that made the impression "A". The illustrations of these impressions have been enlarged two diameters.

The fingerprints of all doctors, sisters, nurses, orderlies, relatives and visitors (642 persons in all) having legitimate access to the ward have been compared with the impressions

If an identification is made, or thought to be made, will you please inform this office and New Scotland Yard before taking any further action?

The letter was also sent to every European police force, in case one of their roving ex-convicts had committed the crime, and then fled the country. Even merchant seamen who had been in the vicinity of Blackburn at the time of the murder were detained when their ships docked at distant ports until they were printed.

But, despite the growing police database, there were no positive results.

Capstick had gambled everything on getting a quick arrest, and he felt in his water that this was the correct strategy. But as May turned into June, and June ebbed into July, and as the number of fingerprints grew from the thousands, to the tens of thousands, he began to fear that something had gone badly wrong.

And then, the investigation ground to a complete halt.

Chapter 16

Breakthrough

Wakes Week is a Northern town tradition, which dated in its earliest form back to the Dark Ages. On the anniversary of the consecration of every church in the land, a 'wake' or holiday would be held, and the locals would be briefly freed from their toil on the land to celebrate. During the industrial revolution, these many holy days interfered with the smooth running of the fledging factories, and so they were consolidated as a regular holiday in the mill towns. The Wake Weeks were an *unpaid* summer holiday, during which all the local industries closed, allowing for maintenance and cleaning. This was quite disruptive when all the towns effectively shut up shop at the same time and so, from 1906, each Lancastrian town had a different nominated fortnight between June and September, where charabancs of workers and their families would go to the new, growing seaside resorts, such as Blackpool and Fleetwood, to divest themselves of the grime and mundanity of industrial life. Staff would contribute to a 'going off' club, where a weekly salary sacrifice would allow them, and their family, to take part in the annual trip. As a result, virtually the entire population of Blackburn began to decamp to coastal climes to partake in the widely believed benefits of sea bathing, bringing the fingerprinting exercise to a grinding halt.

Capstick was kicking his heels in frustration. This was another ghost in his machine. By this time, nearly the whole pool of potential suspects, virtually to the 'last hundred', had been printed and still the killer eluded him. Now, the annual holiday would disrupt his carefully coordinated dragnet, giving the killer even more breathing space. He was also painfully aware that the Farnworth murderer had still not been apprehended, and that the newspapers world-wide were gleefully putting two and two together and making 22.

The press had already begun to dredge the archives for unsolved child murders and write grisly speculative stories suggesting that they were all associated in some way. There was wide theorisation about a 'Moon Killer', a true 'lunatic', who, spurred by the cycles of the satellite, was driven into a murderous monthly frenzy. Capstick himself believed that the Quinten Smith and June Devaney murders were linked, but he did not, at that time, hypothesise further than that. It was also likely that whoever killed Quinten was responsible for the disappearance of Sheila Fox and the attacks on the other girls. Nevertheless, for him there was a difference between facts which supported the 'bleeding obvious', and lurid assumptions. However, in Bolton and Blackburn children were still not being allowed out as they once were and were being escorted in groups to school by parents who took it in turn to guard them. All play was confined to the locality in which they lived under adult supervision. Children found playing alone would be reported to the Police so that they could be returned safely home.

Finally, the deaths became linked to every child disappearance not only in Lancashire, but in the UK. Newspapers referenced each other without checking basic facts, and the theories were wildly exaggerated with each retelling. From Scotland to Cornwall, and ultimately across the world, the media attributed every unfortunate death and disappearance over decades to a mythical single psychopath influenced by the phases of the moon to maim and kill

The whole situation was a powder keg of emotion ready to burst, fuelled by the irresponsible reporting. Perhaps, after all, a vacation was what the town needed to take the heat out of the situation. In the end, Capstick succumbed to pressure from on high to stand down his team for some leave. Resignedly, he rented a cottage for himself, Babs and the kids in Pevensey Bay. The men in his squad followed suit and booked their own holidays.

One by one, they departed, whilst making sure that they each had the phone numbers of the others' destinations in case of unexpected events. Capstick must have been acutely aware that if the Bolton and Blackburn murders were committed by the same man, that another killing could occur at any time, and any delay could be fatal. All the same, he had no choice and reluctantly he began to pack.

Shortly before he was due to leave, he was approached by a pensive Bill Barton. Bill had a lot at stake himself, being in charge of the fingerprinting exercise. There were very few men on the electoral register who had not yet had their fingers painted, and yet the killer had not been found. It was scarcely believable that the murderer would be living in the very last house they would ever approach, and yet, that seemed to be where they were heading. Bill believed that the murderer had slipped through their fingers like smoke, a fact for which he held himself responsible; and had been mulling over how this could have happened. He was not a man who liked bringing problems to his *Guv'nor*. He preferred to present solutions, and he had racked his brains to try and work out what had gone wrong. Finally, he believed he had the answer. Unfortunately, it meant that they might have to start the fingerprinting exercise all over again. He would naturally have been anxious as to how Capstick would respond to such a theory when he broke the bad news.

Capstick demanded to know what exactly he was suggesting when Barton approached him, and he listened incredulously as he explained that the killer might not in fact be on the electoral register after all.

'We know he's young,' Barton said. 'He could be a serving soldier or airman, and in that case, he mightn't show up on the rolls at all.' Capstick was not one for despair, but he must have come near to it as the scales fell from his eyes. They had not found the killer, because, if he had been abroad when the roll was last drafted, he would not have been included and so, effectively, he did not exist on the bureaucratic system they had been using to identify suspects. It must have seemed, even for a brief second, that everything had collapsed away, and that the situation was hopeless. Everything they had done was futile.

Fortunately, Bill had developed a solution, which depended on a different record system.

The Cottontown Killer

Rationing had been introduced several times in the UK during the twentieth century because the British Isles did not produce enough to feed everyone. The limiting of food allowance to every member of the population, whether rich or poor, was particularly inconvenient to the general public, and led to the development of a thriving black market run by desperate and ruthless criminals. However, unpopular as it was, it also is regarded as having improved the general health of the nation. Food rationing during the Second World War began properly in 1940 and continued until 1954. Every member of the population had a ration book, issued by the local Ration Office, where they had to register. Each individual would be categorised according to their weekly need, depending upon whether they were a serviceman or a member of the merchant marine; a civilian; whether they had a manual job, or were unemployed; whether they were pregnant, or whether they had a defined health issue, such as diabetes; and then receive the appropriate calorific and nutritional allowance. The rationing system covered everyone, rich and poor, cradle to grave; and everyone would have a numbered ration book assigned to them. No ration book, no food. If the killer was or had been a serviceman who had recently returned to the town, irrespective of whether he had registered to vote, he would have had to have registered to eat.

'There's a new issue of ration books due,' Barton explained. 'I think it would pay off to check the ration book files against our fingerprint index and see if they tally. Maybe we'll find a few books over.'

In his account of the manhunt, contained in the pamphlet he later wrote with Looms, Campbell outlined the thoroughness of the initial fingerprint run, and the

James Watts & Thomas Watts

developing suspicion as they progressed that there were a substantial number of men who had been missed, and how Barton's new idea was implemented. The local Registration Officer was responsible for issuing and monitoring the distribution of ration books. The latest run of updated books had been published between 30th June and 18th July 1948. To receive a new book, a recipient had to complete a document containing their name, address, and date of birth, along with their Registration Number and old Ration Book. Documentation was filed alphabetically rather than on a 'by street' basis. This meant that the cross referencing of the Ration Book register with the existing Fingerprint Records could be a very lengthy job.

The fingerprinting process was therefore suspended on 18th July, so that the cross referencing could occur. This meant that Campbell and his crew were confined to dealing with the backlog of print records for the three weeks that this took. Each Ration Registration Record had to be compared with the fingerprint cards and the Electoral Register to try and identify if anyone had been previously omitted.

The search revealed a further 200 names of young men who were not contained on the Electoral Roll. Barton and his team were in a position to recommence the systemic fingerprinting of the town on 9th August, focussing on collecting the prints of those who had been left out first time around.

Capstick immediately authorised the new approach and finished his packing over the next few days with a lighter heart, as Barton went back to the registers to compare them with the list of those who was expecting to receive a ration book. The next day he headed for Pevensey Bay for his well-earned sojourn. By his own account, he had barely time to kiss his wife and tousle his boys' hair before the phone rang, summoning him back. It was Looms. 'We've got him,' he said triumphantly.

Capstick rang Mullen who was at Herne Bay, and both men made their own way back to Blackburn, where they were met by Campbell and Looms. Campbell had a card, which contained the prints that were an exact match for those on the bottle. He presented it quietly to Capstick. Job done. *Whatever it takes.*

Chapter 17

46,253

The fingerprints on card designated 46,253 belonged to an ex-Guardsman who lived at 31 Birley Street, with his parents and stepbrother. The house was a nondescript terraced property on a cobbled, dilapidated road. The house had been visited weeks previously during the fingerprint campaign's initial run. However, the youth in question was not on the list that had been given to the visiting officers, and so they were not specifically looking for him. Instead, whilst they stood in the parlour, carefully collecting the fingerprints of the stepbrother, the officers had noticed the sallow, gangly youth who sat at the table playing with matchboxes that he had set up like a small train. They did not take his 'dabs' as his name was not on the list, and it was assumed he would be printed later, when his number came up. However, the young man's name had not been included on the electoral register when it was last updated on 30th June 1947, and so he remained undetected.

He was not so lucky second time around. On 11th August 1948, Officers Calvert and Lamb called and asked specifically for the young man by name and demanded that he surrender his fingerprints as his brother and thousands of others had done before him. He did so without resistance or comment. He could not do otherwise. The card containing the inky ridged patterns was sent to Campbell's team on the same evening.

On 12th August DCI Campbell matched these prints to those on the abandoned Winchester bottle. He informed Looms immediately. As the Yardmen were on leave, it would have been easy to cut them out and initiate the arrest. Looms was not that dishonourable and took the decision that it was only fair that Capstick and his team should be in at the kill. He made the call that brought the Chief Superintendent eagerly back from the shingle beaches of East Sussex to the smoky chimneys of Lancashire.

There must have been a huge feeling of relief that their difficult, some would have said impossible, task was over. All that remained now was to apprehend their target, and to see that justice was done.

Chapter 18

Arrest

Capstick knew this was his moment of triumph, but he also knew that the local officers had worked hard under immense strain, whilst facing increasing criticism, to bring their man to ground. Throughout his autobiography, Capstick makes clear the admiration for officers from Constabulary outside of London who worked hard to keep the peace and solve crime without the resources that he enjoyed. Typically, Capstick decided that the Blackburn Force needed the arrest as much as he did, and specifically included local men in the arrest team. And so, on the morning of Friday 13th August, Capstick, Mullen and Barton were dropped by a squad car outside the red brick terraces of Birley Street. Barton was impatient to barge in and get their man, but Capstick wisely counselled that it was important that the suspect had no opportunity to escape. The young man in question currently had a casual job in a local flour factory as a manual labourer. He left every morning to see if they had work for him. They would lift him in the street as he went.

Shortly after 9am, a slim, tall, tousle haired young chap wearing workman's dungarees over an open necked shirt came out of 31 and began to lope up the street. Capstick knew this man to be guilty of the most terrible crime but noted that he looked no different to any other normal young fellow. Ever one for detail, he remembered later how a lock of dark hair bobbed over his deep set, shadowed eyes as he walked along. Up, and down. Up, and down. Up. Down.

After all the effort, all the time invested, it was finally time to close the trap. The policemen started walking, matched the youth's speed, caught up with him, and made their move. Capstick caught hold of his arm, whilst Mullen boxed him in. They let Barton feel his collar.

'Peter Griffiths,' Barton intoned, 'we are police officers, and I am going to arrest you for the murder of June Ann Devaney at Queen's Park Hospital on the night of 14th-15th of May this year. I must warn you that anything you say may be taken down in writing and given in evidence.'

Griffiths stared at Barton, and then blankly looked around at each of the officers in turn. There was no escape. It seemed an age, but in fact it can only have been seconds before he spoke. 'What's it to do with me? I've never been near the place.'

The squad car reappeared, and Capstick nodded towards the back seat. Passively, Griffiths got in next to him. Mullen sat in the front, alongside Chief Superintendent Woodmansey, who was driving. A second car picked up Barton, who would actually be credited with the arrest. The car made its way towards the station in Northgate. No one spoke, and the tension must have been unbearable. Eventually, Griffiths said 'I've never been in any ward at Queen's Park Hospital. But I used to play in the Delph when I was a lad.'

Capstick's only reply was to repeat the police caution. Again, the journey continued in silence. Griffiths must have been in a blue funk, his mind working furiously. Again, he broke the silence. 'Is it...is it my fingerprints, why you've come to me?'

Capstick looked him in the eye and repeated the caution for a third time before answering. 'Yes.'

By this time, they had arrived at Northgate. Woodmansey parked outside the imposing facade of the station, and they stepped out on the pavement. Capstick and Mullen flanked Griffiths, who stared up at the building before they walked him into the main entrance. Griffiths paused as they entered, and, resigned, finally said 'Well, if they are my fingerprints on the bottle, I'll tell you all about it.'

Chapter 19

Interrogation

Although Capstick was canny enough to allow Blackburn Borough Constabulary to get their fair credit for the arrest of Peter Griffiths, he took charge of the interrogation himself. There were several reasons for this. Firstly, this was Scotland Yard's show, and whilst an arrest was a 'result', they needed to secure the conviction. Capstick knew that local feelings were running high, and the Yard did not want a clever defence lawyer to seize on any irregularity that could invalidate a trial. A hot-headed local plod dishing out his own brand of instant justice could ensure that Griffiths actually walked free. The local force would therefore be involved, but Capstick would make sure the charges would stick. Whilst he would not go as far as to count how many teeth the prisoner arrived with, he would make sure that Griffiths would not meet with an unfortunate accident whilst in custody. At least, not one where the bruises would show.

Today, prisoner interviews are timed, recorded, filmed and available for review in Court, in evidence and even on reality TV. We know who said what, and in what tone; we can see their body language, the subtle nuances of unspoken communication that convey so much; we can see exactly when the accused breaks and confesses all, or the moment when the steel shines in their eyes and they sneer 'no comment'. No such methods of recording existed in 1948, and even full transcripts of interrogations were rarely taken. Often, the only thing written down was the confession, if one resulted, or a modified summary of the questioning, even if that questioning lasted hours, or days. However, we actually know a lot about Capstick's standard method of interrogation because it came under significant scrutiny many years after his death, in relation to the both celebrated, and later infamous, conviction of Iain Hay Gordon.

What was to be Capstick's most infamous case began in the early hours of 13th November 1952 with a phone call to the Royal Ulster Constabulary at Whiteabbey Barracks, Belfast, from Glen House, the home of Judge Lancelot Curran. The Judge was raising concern about his flighty daughter's worrying absence.

Constable Rutherford was despatched to the scene on his bicycle and arrived at the Judge's home at the same time as Davison, the Judge's pet solicitor. Patricia Curran, the Judge's daughter, lay on the drive her head being cradled by her brother Desmond. Despite her family's assertions, she was obviously clearly dead at this time. She had been stabbed so many times in the face that at first it was thought that she had been peppered at close range with shotgun pellets. At some point, the evidence showed, Patricia had dropped her university work, and either she, or her assailant, had taken the time to stack it up neatly on the grass. Patricia's dress and underwear had been disturbed, but she had not been raped. The Judge spotted Rutherford, and immediately pulled rank. He claimed that his daughter was still alive, and that they were taking her for immediate medical treatment. Rutherford, intimidated as he was by the Judge's intervention, could only watch helplessly as the family and the solicitor took Patricia away in Davison's car.

Rutherford called for assistance and did his best to secure what was left the crime scene before reporting to his superiors. Curran was highly connected, and had immense influence, both personally and politically. The Northern Ireland of the time was, as always, a tumultuous and dangerous place. Much of Ireland had been fighting for centuries to be an independent country rather than an English fiefdom, and its population had a long and detailed recollection of oppression, famine and disenfranchisement. The Uprising of Easter '16 was still a real memory, as was the bloody civil war that resulted from the formation of the embryonic Free State. The majority of the country was properly independent by 1937 and declared a formal Republic in 1949. This was not the end of the violence, however because the largely protestant north remained a part of the United Kingdom. Sectarian and political differences, centring on the 6 states of Ulster resulted in an internecine, and increasingly bitter, war of attrition between loyalist and nationalist parties, and their various, vicious splinter factions. Although officially neutral in the Second World War, the Republic did little to prevent the IRA's campaigns on the British mainland. The early 1950's was somewhat quiescent, as the IRA raided various police and army depots in an attempt to arm itself for its coming campaign. In 1953, however, the political temperature would rise rapidly due to a combination of local and world events. In January several prominent northern Irish politicians perished when the ferry *MV Princess Victoria* went down on its trip from Stranraer; later, the Republic's Taoiseach, de Valera, would call for the return of the remains of the hero- or traitor-(depending on your viewpoint)- of Sir Roger Casement; and prior to the Coronation of the new Queen Elizabeth II, who would visit the Province later in the year, US President FDR would deliberately pour petrol on the fire by demanding that the US Senate support a motion calling for a united Ireland.

Given the highly charged environment, an attack on the family of a highly valued and politically important establishment Judge was an issue which required attention from the highest level. Consequently, Capstick, who had coincidentally been on holiday in Dublin, had his leave cancelled and was seconded to supervise the investigation.

The case was both straightforward, and baffling. 19-year-old Patricia Doris Curran had last been seen in the company of her boyfriend, John Steel, before getting the 5pm bus to the stop near her home. At 5.45pm, newspaper delivery-boy George Chapman had heard some loud rustling in the undergrowth lining the drive up to the Glen, but had been unable to ascertain the cause.

There were no obvious clues until the RAF Special Investigation Branch, which had been asked to question airmen and civilian workers at the nearby HQ of 67 Group, Fighter Command, notified the RUC of a suspect. Skinny, isolated and shy, Leading Airman Gordon was a gift for the police. Capstick described him as slim, educated and religious, and in many ways 'too good to be true'. He had been identified as being in the vicinity of the Glen at the time of the murder by two independent witnesses. Gordon, who admitted to being acquainted with the Currans through Desmond, had originally provided a reasonable alibi. However, it was then found that he had asked several colleagues to vouch for his whereabouts when they had not been with him. Gordon was seen to be sporting a black eye, and there was found to be some blood on his trousers.

The police were then approached by Desmond Curran who claimed to have been enticed into a conversation by Gordon, during which he continued to talk about his sister's murder, claiming that she had been killed by the fourth blow of the assault. They convinced Desmond to engage Gordon in further phone conversations, which they listened in to.

Gordon was finally arrested on January 13th 1953. Capstick claimed that Gordon was interrogated by the RUC, with he himself seeing him only briefly on a couple of occasions. His assertion was challenged during the trial, particularly his interrogation technique, which concentrated on Gordon's sexuality. For example, his notebook record of the interviews states:

"10.20 am, the 15/1/53, saw Gordon at office. Dist. Inspr. Nelson left him and I questioned him at length re masturbation, gross indecency, sodomy"

Capstick claimed that it was necessary for Gordon to be interrogated extensively about his homosexuality, which was at that time a criminal offence; only because if he was honest about that, it meant they could trust whatever else he told them was true. He confirmed to the trial Judge, that he did not concentrate on this aspect merely to intimidate him. In his memoirs, he wrote:

'...I had to make that boy tell me the truth about his private life and most secret thoughts. Only then could I begin to believe him she he began to tell the truth about Patricia Curran. I hated to use what might well seem to be ruthless measures. I was never sorrier for any criminal than for that unhappy, maladjusted youngster. But his mask had to be broken.'

Capstick stated that he merely reviewed Gordon's statements with him, and accused him of lying, at which point Gordon blurted out 'Did anyone see me leaving the Glen?', before claiming that he must have murdered Patricia whilst in a blackout. Capstick and the RUC claimed that Gordon gave his subsequent confession as one long stream of consciousness, which Capstick transcribed as it was dictated. It clearly described how the books ended up neatly piled on the path but was vague on the actual attack.

According to the RUC, after signing the confession, Hays wrote in his own hand:

'I am very sorry for having killed Patricia Curran. I had no intention whatsoever of killing the girl. It was solely due to a black-out. God knows as well as anybody else that the furthest thing in my mind was to kill the girl and I ask His forgiveness. I throw myself on to the mercy of

*the law and I ask you to do your best for me so
that I can make a complete restart in life. I
should like to say how sorry I am for all the
distress that I have caused the Curran family. I
have felt run down for quite some time and the
black-out may have been the result of over-
studying and worry generally. I am also sorry for
the distress and worry I have caused my dear
father and mother. I ask my parents' forgiveness
and if I am spared, I shall redeem my past life.'*

The Prosecution case was therefore that Gordon, the
closet homosexual, was suddenly overtaken with lust for the
19-year-old girl, and when his clumsy attempt at satisfying
this urge was thwarted, he killed her in his frenzy. To be
objective, there was other evidence apart from Gordon's
statement that was relevant to the conviction. There was for
example the blood on his trousers; and although it was never
identified as the murder weapon, a stiletto type letter opener,
found on a beach, was handed in. It was similar to a knife
which had gone missing from an office in the RAF base, an
office to which Gordon had access.

Gordon was found guilty, but escaped death because the
he was judged to have been momentarily insane. He was
released in 1960 and lived anonymously in Glasgow,
although he continued to campaign for a full pardon into the
21st Century. His appeal was finally heard in 2000, during
which he gave his own version of how he was interrogated.
The Judges concluded that Capstick had put immense
psychological pressure on Gordon, and that the RUC had
extensively intimidated him. Gordon later claimed that

Capstick wrote the confession and he, exhausted beyond endurance, signed it without reading it. Gordon later gave his version as to how the interview was conducted.

'.. *I was in a small room, say 12ft by 8ft. There were four police officers on one side and I was on the other. From about 2 o'clock till 10 they were shouting non-stop at me, "You did it, you did it, you did it.''...They said the shock [of homosexual activity] would kill [my mother]...Every time I opened my mouth they said, "You're a liar, you're a liar, you're a liar. If you don't confess you'll go to hell." ... they gave me hardly anything to eat and drink. I was exhausted, shattered. I think if I hadn't signed that statement, I would have thrown myself out of that window to get some peace.... For a while I didn't know whether I'd killed Patricia Curran or not because of the state of my mind. Gradually when I came to my senses, in the prison and in the hospital, I realised I hadn't killed her.'*

He described Capstick's tactics in detail.

'.. *He played a sort of fantasy game, saying, "Suppose you had met Patricia Curran. Would you have walked her up the drive?" And he wrote that up as "He walked her up the drive". The whole thing was Capstick's invention. "Would you stop to give her a kiss?" That went down as "He stopped to give Curran a kiss..."*

The Appeal was upheld, and 47 years after he was convicted, Gordon received his pardon. The Judges were critical of Capstick's conduct and ruled that the confession should have been 'inadmissible'. Capstick, of course, was not there to defend himself, but there were other important matters which also went in Gordon's favour. The trial Judge's summing up was found to be biased; the forensic evidence, including the estimated time of death, were found to be questionable; the evidence of an 11-year-old girl who had seen Patricia in the company of an unknown, scarred man, was not presented. More astonishingly, during psychiatric assessment Gordon had been subjected to sodium pentothal therapy in an attempt to retrieve lost memories. The Appeal Court found that this treatment was just as likely to lead to the creation of false memories, and so this evidence should also not have been allowed.

Patricia Curran's murder therefore is now unsolved, but there are many theories, which, given the peculiar behaviour of the family on the night in question, generally involve a conspiracy to secure stability in the Ulster judicial system.

The importance of this episode, if Gordon's evidence can be taken at face value, is that it gives a fairly unique insight into how a detective like Capstick got a confession. Clearly, he put a lot of unorthodox psychological pressure on the suspect, which probably arose from his experiences with real career criminals rather than sad and vulnerable young men. The niceties of exploring motives were all very well, but he was clearly a believer in the direct approach and was not one to let inconvenient facts get in the way of a good hunch. It is clear from his autobiography that Capstick sincerely believed that Gordon had killed Patricia Curran and that the quickest and easiest way to clear up the crime now that they had a suspect was to get a confession. And that is what he set out to do.

Let us wind back now, to 1948. There is Peter Griffiths, a strange and lonely young man, with few friends, who suffered from crippling social awkwardness. Basically, a tortured boy in a man's body, who had not properly mentally matured to adulthood despite having fought for his country. His family was dysfunctional and marred by insanity. He himself, emotionless, blank, a cypher, now a child molester and murderer, for there was no doubt that Griffiths had killed the girl after horrifically assaulting her. There was no need to go into motive: that was for head-shrinkers, psychologists and left-wing namby-pamby apologists. The evidence was indisputable. What was important was to get the culprit bang to rights, just to tie things up airtight with a nice little confession. Not enough detail to upset the parents mind, but enough to see him swiftly to the gallows.

Perhaps it is significant that Capstick sent Detective Sergeant Mullen outside the room to get some paper and pens, leaving him alone with Griffiths for an undisclosed period of time. Or maybe we should not read anything into it at all. We can imagine the scene, though. Griffiths sat across the desk from Capstick and the Blackburn officers. The room, dark, probably clouded with smoke, the men hot and sweaty, like their tempers. Perhaps they are in shirt sleeves and braces, sometimes shouting, sometimes friendly, the threat of blistering violence not far away; Griffiths removed, saying little, as if focussed on something else. And then, Capstick tries a different approach, like that of a stern, but well meaning, father. Perhaps stuffing tobacco into his big bowled pipe and lighting it. C'mon lad, we know you did it. You know it, and you know we can prove it. You can have it the hard way, but why not make it easy for yourself? Why put the poor girl's family through the agony of a prolonged trial? Why drag out their pain more than you have to? We know you're good at heart. You couldn't help yourself. It was the drink, maybe. Or perhaps the killer's moon influenced you? Think of her parents. Think of your own. Think of yourself. The only thing you can do for them now is be a man, face up to what you have done, and make it easier for them all. Think, think, think of the mothers...

Unsurprisingly it was only a short period of time before Griffiths signed a confession. Perhaps he realised it was hopeless. Perhaps he genuinely wanted to atone in some way. Perhaps he did not know what he was signing. Perhaps, perhaps, perhaps he just did not care one way or the other. In any event, Peter Griffiths then apparently dictated a statement that was carefully written down by Mullen in Capstick's presence. Griffiths then signed every page of the document which would become Exhibit 8 at his trial, and which would seal his fate, if it were ever in doubt.

Chapter 20

Confession

I want to say that on the night the little girl was killed at Queen's Park Hospital, it was a Friday night, the Friday before Whitsun. I left home that night on my own about six o'clock. I went out to spend a quiet night on my own. I went to the *Dun Horse* pub or hotel and bought myself about five pints of bitter beer, then I went to *Yates' Wine Lodge* and had a glass of Guinness and two double rums. I then had another glass of Guinness and then went back to the *Dun Horse* again. I then had about six more pints of bitter, I was on my own and came out of there at closing time. I walked down to Jubilee Street off Darwen Street, and I saw a man smoking a cigarette sitting in a small closed car with the hood on, with wire wheels, they were painted silver. I did not know him, I had never seen him before, I asked the man for a light as I had no matches to light my cigarette. I stayed gabbing to him for about fifteen minutes, he said to me 'Are you going home?' I said 'No, I'm going to walk round a bit and sober up first.' He asked me where I lived and I told him. He said 'Well get in, open the window and I'll give you a spin.' He took me to the front of Queen's Park Hospital and I got out opposite to the iron railings. I don't know what happened to him again. I must have got over the railings, but the next thing I remember was being outside the ward where there was some children. I left my shoes outside a door which had a brass knob, I tried the door and it opened to my touch and I just went in and I heard a nurse humming and banging things as if she was washing something so I came out again and waited a few minutes. Then I went back in again and went straight to the ward like, I think I went in one or two small rooms like, and then came back into the ward again. I then picked up a biggish bottle off a shelf. I went halfway down the ward with it and then put it down on the floor, I then thought I heard the nurse coming, I turned round sharply, over balanced and fell against a bed. I remember the child woke up and started to cry and I hushed her, she then opened her eyes and saw me and the child in the next bed started whimpering. I picked up the girl out of the cot and took her outside by the same door. I carried her in my right arm, and she put her arms around my neck, and I walked with her down the hospital field. I put her down on the grass. She started crying again, and I tried to stop her from crying, but she wouldn't do like, she wouldn't stop crying. I just lost my temper and you know what happened then. I banged her head against the wall. I then went back to the veranda outside the ward, sat down and put my shoes on. I then went back to where the child was. I like just glanced at her but did not go right up to her but went straight down the field to the Delph. I crossed over the path alongside the Delph leading into Queen's Park. I walked through the Park and came out on Audley. I went down Cherry Street into Furthergate, then I went down Eanam to Birley Street and got home somewhere about two o'clock on Saturday morning. It would be somewhere about that time, I went into me house, took me collar and tie off and slept in me suit on the couch downstairs. Mother and father were in bed and did not know what time I came in. I woke up about nine o'clock, got up, washed and shaved, and then pressed me suit because I was going out again after I had had my breakfast. I went out then down the town, had a walk round and then went to the Royal cinema afternoon, came out of the pictures at five o'clock, and went home and had my tea. I looked at the paper and read about the murder, it didn't shake me so that I just carried on normally after that. My mother and father asked me where I had been that night and what time I came home and I told them I had been out boozing and had got home at twelve o'clock. This is all I can say and I'm sorry for both parents' sake and I hope I get what I deserve.

Chapter 21

The Strange, Enchanted Boy

Now the police had their man, they could dig into his background and search his haunts for clues to make the case more concrete. One of the key missing forensic items was the suit that Griffiths wore on the night of the killing. When arrested, he was wearing overalls and a shirt. His only other clothing was his battledress. His de-mob suit was nowhere to be found. However, a diligent search of his room revealed a pawn shop ticket. When the police attended the shop, there was the suit, waiting to be redeemed. Off it went to Campbell's men at Hutton.

Griffith's bedroom revealed other colourful items. For example, there were several scrapbooks containing pictures of animals cut from magazines, along with pictures of celebrities, collated, filed, obviously repeatedly examined and perused, but with no clue as to why.

There was little else to find, really. Griffiths shared the bedroom with his elder stepbrother, using it in shifts. What else was there would be hopelessly compromised and would just be useful for background information. The investigation began to concentrate more on tracing witnesses and contacts: family, friends, girlfriends; health professionals and army commanders. Slowly, Griffith's extraordinary background began to be revealed. His father was a known schizophrenic, following his experiences in the Great War. Griffiths himself had suffered a major head injury as a child. He later spent two years-*two years!* -as an inpatient in CH3 ward with a non-specific neurotic illness that manifested as enuresis (bed wetting). He had few if any adult friends, preferring to play with children, particularly a niece, his stepbrother's daughter. Otherwise, he was generally solitary, playing child's games with matchboxes. Called up for the second war, he had a non-descript military career, interspersed with periods of desertion. All of this gave a glimpse into the mind of the man who had become a child killer. But perhaps the clue that was most suggestive was the poem, written in his own poor handwriting and containing his own eccentric spelling, that had been pinned to his bedroom wall:

WARNING
For lo and behold, when the beast
Look down on the face of beuty
It staids its hand from Killing
And from that day on
It were as one dead
–   The Terror

Chapter 22

The Queer Woman

Once it became clear that the Blackburn child murderer was in custody, the country breathed a sigh of relief, and the restrictions that had been placed upon children were relaxed. Life began to slowly return to normality.

One would think that Griffiths arrest would keep all other news out of the headlines for a period of time. Unfortunately, this was not to be the case, as the papers were handed an incredibly juicy story a few days after he was initially put away, which took place virtually next door.

Rawtenstall is a small village, about 12 miles south of Blackburn, on the way to Bury. It is nestled on the banks of the River Irwell, which rolls from its origin in the village of

Bacup towards the Mersey, acting as the boundary between Salford and Manchester on the way. In the early hours of 22nd August, the body of an elderly woman, Nancy Chadwick, was found lying on the main road by the driver of the Number 46 bus, Herbert Beaumont. So badly injured was she that initially it was thought she had been the victim of a hit-and-run. However, it was found that she had been dead over ten hours. Medical examination confirmed that her head had been stove in by repeated blows with a hammer. Witnesses confirmed that the body could only have been placed in the road between 03:45 and 04:00. Someone therefore had stored her body somewhere and dumped her in the road in the middle of the night.

As is often the way in these tales of murder, suspicion centred on a woman regarded as a local eccentric partly because of her bizarre nature, and partly because she just could not help drawing attention to herself

Today, Margaret Allen would have been able to live her life as a lesbian, or trans-gender person without much of a raised eyebrow. She would also have had access to the psychological and medical support that she so clearly needed for her mental health issues. In harder, less enlightened times she never really stood a chance. She was the *twentieth* child of 22 and had lived with her mother until her death in 1943. She then moved into 137 Bacup Road, a tiny little cottage. She spent most of her life in poverty, lurching from one low paid job to another between spells of unemployment. For many years, she dressed as a man, and insisted on being addressed as 'Bill'. In August 1948, she was at risk of being evicted having lost the job she loved as a bus conductor after a fit of temper. Nancy Chadwick, a fussy busybody, who usually dressed in Victorian clothes and often put on odd shoes, had become acquainted with Margaret at the beginning of August, by repeatedly nagging her to lend her a cup of sugar. On the 21st, she effectively barged her way into Margaret's home, despite best efforts to prevent her. Margaret later described how she had been in one of her 'funny moods' and, unable to take any more of the chatterbox's incessant talk, she grabbed the first thing to hand and smacked the woman over the head, repeatedly, until she stopped moving. Once the frenzy had passed, Margaret went about her normal business for the day after pushing the dead woman in the coalhouse. She intended to tip her into the nearby Irwell in the middle of the night. However, she was not strong enough, and so left the body in the road, just outside of her house. Which, to be honest, should have been a bit of a giveaway to the Lancashire Constabulary, although it did not appear to be a significant clue to the authorities at first. Instead of keeping her head down, Margaret kept pestering the searching police, claiming to have located Chadwick's bag which she herself had disposed of in the river, and offering to identify the dead woman. Having been questioned twice, and having had her house searched, she finally confessed to Inspector Stevens.

A strange, cross dressing woman, who battered an inoffensive matriarch to death? It was made for the tabloids; and the headlines made a great and timely diversion from the other local matter that was not progressing. Griffiths fell out of the news, and Margaret Allen was projected into the limelight, the new star act in the northern media freak show.

Chapter 23

The Sea Monster

The Houses of Parliament, Westminster
June – July 1948

The abolitionists had only a small time to celebrate their victory in having the death penalty suspended. The House of Lords, the non-elected Chamber of the British Parliament, debated the Bill on 1st and 2nd June. The arguments were re-examined, but the Peers are notoriously conservative, and so the arguments to get them to act against their natures and challenge the Government by sending a Bill back would have to be convincing. However, the subject of crime and punishment is always evocative, and there were many in the House who felt that the Commons had gone against the will of the people in passing the Bill in the first place. The dilemma for the Government Peers reflected that of the Commons MPs: if they supported the Bill, they would be enacting the will of Parliament, but would be embarrassing the Government, perhaps fatally. If they did not pass the Bill, the Government would be defeated, another crushing and unneeded blow. In addition, however, the opposition Peers were looking for an excuse to sow mischief and embarrass the ruling Party. The scene was set for a major struggle.

Firstly, it was argued that the majority *for* abolition in the House of Commons was actually greater than had been recorded in April, for technical reasons. Essentially, as the Government had declared a free vote, Ministers, who might be in favour of abolition, were obliged to abstain. It was virtually certain that they would vote in favour next time, so that the majority in favour of the Bill would inevitably increase. It was also argued that most murderers were victims of impulse and so *could not* be deterred whatever the penalty; whereas habitual recidivists who casually murdered for their own ends *would not* be deterred. It was therefore unlikely that the death penalty prevented any killings, particularly as statistics showed that only a minority of convicted killers who had their sentences commuted, and were later released on license, ever reoffended. If one were to believe the experience of other countries, abolition also did not lead to any increase in any violent crimes. The debate was fiercely fought, but despite these powerful facts, the Bill was eventually defeated by an overwhelming majority, and was returned to the Commons for a second debate.

The second Commons debate was not allowed to touch on current police investigations, and so the Blackburn Baby Murder was not mentioned. However, there was a large amount of public concern about the case of PC Nathanial Edgar, shot dead in February whilst questioning David Thomas in connection with a string of robberies. When arrested, Thomas had gone for his gun, confessing that he had intended to shoot the officers. He was tried in April, but, due to the suspension of the death penalty, received life imprisonment. Surely such a ruthless murderer should not escape the gallows? In the event, Thomas would be released 14 years later. Another notorious case known as the Porthole Murder, was frequently alluded to during the debate. This concerned the disappearance of young actress Gay Gibbons from the *SS Durban Castle*. It is worth relating the details of the case, so that the intensity of the feelings raised by the debate can be accurately reflected.

Gibbons, 21, a young woman of stunning good looks, had enjoyed some success in a touring company in South Africa, but was returning to the UK to pursue her career. During the trip she was often escorted by two older men, Frank Hopwood, an official of the shipping line, and Wing Commander Bray. The ship was not full, and there was not much company, and so Gay often allowed Bray and Hopwood to squire her chivalrously to her room at the end of the day. Unfortunately for her, she also struck up a friendly rapport with Ship's Deck Steward James Camb. Camb, 31, a married father of one daughter, had spent most of his adult life at sea. He was a notorious lothario and was unpopular with the rest of the crew. Ruggedly handsome, he had narrowly escaped losing his job on more than one occasion because of his amorous pursuits. Camb preyed almost exclusively on lonely and vulnerable women, and recently, three had found themselves molested by him on previous trips. One had survived being strangled when she resisted his advances. None made an official complaint, for fear they would get a reputation as a 'loose woman', and so Camb remained employed. This information only came out after his trial.

On 17th October 1947, Gibbons was escorted to her room as usual, but was later seen on deck, complaining that she could not sleep because she was too warm. She was then seen having a brief conversation with Camb, during which he gently scolded her for not consuming the drink she had ordered from him the night before. Later that evening, the two bells signalling that assistance was required from both the Cabin Steward and the Stewardess, were sounded from her cabin, B126. The steward attended but caught a glimpse only of the back of a man in singlet and trousers who informed him that everything was okay before slamming the door in his face. He recognised this man as Camb. The next morning, Gay was noticed to be missing, as were her pyjamas and dressing gown. There were slight bloodstains found on her bed.

The ship was searched, but no trace of her could be found. Captain Patey sent out an SOS to other ships that might be in the area, and even briefly turned the boat around, trying to retrace their path in a desperate attempt to find her. Sadly, it was soon realised that if she had gone overboard, she would have fallen into the sea over ninety miles from land, in shark infested waters. All hope was lost. There was no doubt that Gay Gibbons was dead.

The captain was then informed of the strange alarm call to her cabin. Camb was summoned and seen, unusually for the tropics, to be wearing a long-sleeved jacket, rather than a short-sleeved shirt. He was also found to have scratches on his arms, and neck. At first, he denied everything, but when the ship docked he remained the main suspect, and was interviewed by the police. It was only when Detective Sergeant Quinlan suggested that the cause of Gay's demise may not necessarily have been sinister, that Camb cracked. He claimed that she had invited him to her room for the purpose of sex. When he arrived, she wore only a flimsy dressing gown, and had invited him to bed. During intercourse, she had suffered a seizure, and died. He tried desperately to resuscitate her but failed. When his colleague came to the door, Camb panicked, and forced the lifeless body out of the porthole into the sea below. Unsurprisingly, Camb was arrested for murder. During another interview, he allegedly let slip that he was surprised that the ship's watchman had not noticed the 'hell of a noise' when the girl's body hit the water. His turn of phrase during this offhand statement also suggested that she had struggled when forced through the porthole, the terrible implication being that she had in fact been alive when ejected from the ship. To be fair, this evidence had been given by one Officer Plumley, whom, it was suspected, had been allowed to suddenly retire from the police rather than face some sort of disciplinary matter.

Camb stuck to his story, seemingly believing that he would not be found guilty if there was no body to be found. The evidence however was overwhelming. It was suggested by the prosecution that Camb actually came uninvited into the cabin, and forced himself on the girl, who resisted. Camb had strangled her to keep her quiet. During the struggle, she had probably pressed both the alarm bells which were near the bed. It was this event for which Camb never had any explanation that weighed heavily against him. Why would both alarms have been pressed if not as part of a desperate attempt to summon help during a life or death battle? The bed sheets were found to be stained with blood that was not Camb's group, and urine. If the blood was not Camb's, then it must have been the girl's. Expert evidence was that the passing of a large amount of urine was consistent with violent death, such as strangulation. Camb's credibility was destroyed by a careful cross examination, during which he agreed that he had not consistently told the truth. Beastly behaviour, he was forced to admit. The defence, on the other hand, had no option but to attack the girl's reputation, in order to support Camb's story that she had seduced him. In addition, witnesses from her time in South Africa, and from when she served in the WRACs, were called to give evidence that she had some undiagnosed underlying health condition that could cause sudden seizures. However, Camb could not explain why, if his story was true that she had truly died of natural causes, that he had disposed of the body rather than let it be found in the morning. This went down badly with the jury and the public, who regarded him as callous and unfeeling. Even if his story was true, for all he knew, the woman could have been saved had help been summoned. He was found guilty and sentenced to death. However, due to the hiatus on the death penalty, this was commuted to life imprisonment. There was a public outcry, due to the feeling that a particularly heartless murderer and raper of women had escaped justice. This case was used frequently during the Parliamentary discussion to illustrate the argument against abandoning the death penalty.

In the end, James Camb served 11 years in total and was released on license in 1959. He changed his name to Clarke and became a waiter. He always protested his innocence, but a leopard cannot really change its spots. In 1967, he was found to have attempted to seduce a 13 year-old girl, but was-astonishingly-not returned to prison, receiving only a 2 years further probation. Later, a series of child grooming and molestation offences were uncovered, and he was finally sent back to jail. He was released in 1978, and died a well-earned ghastly death from heart failure in 1979

Meantime, in the debate, the great Churchill was particularly vocal. He ridiculed Home Secretary Ede, the abolitionists and, indeed, the initial decision to allow a free vote at all. That, he snarled, was the sign of a Government which was afraid to show real leadership.

The end result was that a mishmash of defeated amendments and unhappy compromises were progressively added to the Abolition Bill. For example, it was proposed that murders would fall into different categories, but that poisoners would *always* face death penalty. Attempts to modify this point were scathingly dissected in that, if the law changed as purported, a poisoner who killed someone over a long-term period would face the death penalty, but someone who killed a victim with a toxin in one dose would not. It was also suggested that the amendments meant that the killer of a police officer would always face the noose; but if the same murderer killed a member of the public who was assisting the officer, they would not. These logistical conflicts were used to mercilessly excoriate the Government.

Factors such as this were central in the ultimate failure of the Bill when it was returned to the Lords in July. The Bill was once more thrown out, having been condemned in Parliament and the press as a 'murderer's code'. In August 1948, therefore, the Government finally gave up and the death penalty was reactivated. The issue was bounced back for another Royal Commission report which would not conclude until 1949.

Having come so near to have achieving their goal, the abolitionists now faced bitter disappointment. The earlier Royal Commission that had initially reported in their favour had been ignored; the 5-year proposal to suspend the death penalty had been roundly defeated; and this latest Commission did not have the terms of reference that would allow it to produce a result that they would accept as reasonable. The matter was now firmly in the long grass, where it would stay for nearly twenty long years. Silverman had gambled, gambled it all, and lost, badly. It is unclear whether the terrible murder that had occurred in a constituency neighbouring his played a major part in this turn of fortune. It is unlikely that its influence was insignificant.

The importance of this outcome to the town of Blackburn was very clear. The murderer of June Ann Devaney, had he been put on trial between April and August 1948 would like Camb not have faced the death penalty for his heinous, unspeakable actions. Now, if he were to be found guilty, execution was firmly back on the agenda.

Chapter 24

The First Day

Lancaster
15th October 1948

Despite the weight of evidence, and the damning confession, the trial of Peter Griffiths was not to go uncontested.

The proceedings were scheduled to take place on Friday 15th October 1948, at Lancaster Assizes, overshadowed by the impressive mediaeval castle that was the heart of the city, the same castle at which the unfortunate Pendle Witches, and others, had faced their terrible fates.

Griffiths was transported there from jail, and then held in the cells underneath the castle. It was during one of these trips that Ernie Mullen claimed to have stopped Griffiths attempting suicide by eating glass. There is no other record of Griffiths displaying any other sort of emotion during the trial.

When Mr Justice Oliver, the respected Judge, signalled that he was ready to start, Griffiths was taken into the dock where he was guarded by several large men, his pale, thin face looking across the large room, its public gallery packed with members of the press and curious members of the public.

British justice is a mixture of procedure and guignol theatre, characterised by battles of wits that decided the freedom or imprisonment of culprits, their ultimate fate depending on a turn of phrase or the emphasis of an individual word in an exchange between bewigged and gowned intellectuals. On this occasion the protagonists were W. Gorman KC, Barrister at Law and Mr D. Brabin , instructed by the Director of Public Prosecutions; and Basil Nield and J.V. Nahum for the defence, instructed by Holden, Blanthorne and Daies Solicitors, Blackburn. They took their places, exchanged pleasantries, and knowing looks, shuffled papers. The faces in the public gallery turned to the prisoner, furtive glances as the players in the pantomime took their seats. When Justice Oliver arrived, everyone stood, on pain of Contempt of Court. When sitting in Judgement, he represented the King, and needed to be paid the appropriate respect. When he sat in the huge throne behind the bench, everyone else was finally allowed to sit also. The Clerk of The Court then stood and addressed the Prisoner in the Dock. In a clear voice so that everyone could hear, he said: 'Peter Griffiths, you are indicted and the charge against you is murder; in that you, on the 15th May, 1948, at Blackburn in the County of Lancaster, murdered June Anne Devaney. How say you, Peter Griffiths? Are you guilty? Or not guilty?'

Peter Griffiths, standing, dwarfed by his guards, but due to the prominence of the dock, on clear view to all, said in reply, barely audible, 'Not guilty.'

These were to be the only words he ever spoke at the trial.

Given the weight and depth of evidence against him, it may seem a curious plea. However, Griffiths was on trial for his life. Following a guilty plea, the Judge would have been required to remind him that the only sentence that could be applied was the death penalty and that unless he changed his plea, it would be immediately ordered. He would then encourage him, and his Counsel, strongly to reconsider. On occasion, if the accused insisted on a guilty plea, it was not unknown for defence counsel to inform the judge that the client was not fit to plead, which would lead to the trial going ahead anyway. It was not in this case going to be argued that Griffiths was unfit to plead, but rather that he was not deserving of the death penalty, because he was insane when he committed the crime. A *not guilty* plea would allow them to explore not whether Griffiths did the murder, but if he was not in control of his faculties whilst he did it.

The legal definition of insanity was not easy to fulfil, and had its roots in the assassination of Edward Drummond, private secretary to Sir Robert Peel, in 1843.

Daniel M'Naghten, a wood turner and sometime actor from Glasgow had developed the ideation that he was being persecuted by the Government. He became increasingly paranoid, and, on 20th January 1843, he shot Drummond five times in the back in broad daylight. He was eventually found not guilty on the grounds of insanity. The resulting public, and Royal, outrage led to five Judges being asked to justify the verdict. Their answers were later enshrined as the 'M'Naghten Rules':

> *To establish a defence on the ground of insanity it must be clearly proved, that, at the time of committing the act, the party accused was labouring under such a defect of reason from disease of the mind, as not to know the nature and quality of the act he was doing, or if he did know it, that he did not know that what he was doing was wrong*

Therefore, the trial would be fought on the grounds as to whether Griffiths knew what he was doing at the point that he abducted and murdered a 3-year-old girl was wrong. If it could be shown, beyond a reasonable doubt, that he did, he would hang; if he did not, he would be confined at His Majesty's Pleasure, probably indefinitely, in one of the judicial insane asylums maintained for this very purpose.

The decision would therefore rest not on the facts of the crime, but the medical and family history of the criminal; the results of medical examinations; and whether there was evidence of premeditation or planned evasion.

The presentation of evidence by Mr Gorman started with what was referred to as 'evidence after the fact'. That is, confirmation as to who was dead, where they were found, and the environment surrounding the events. Taylor and Sherlock, the police photographers, and Detective Sergeant Bowden who mapped the crime scene gave their accounts to an impassive courtroom. They showed the court the graphic photographs and maps that they had made of the scene.

They were followed into the stand by Nurse Humphreys, who had been photographed arriving at the Court in the company of Albert Devaney. He had looked unsurprisingly haggard and gaunt, she prim, proper and professional. Nurse Humphreys spent some considerable time being encouraged to describe the layout of the wards and the position of the cots with the help of diagrams provided to her. She had to re-enact her movements on the night in question in great detail, which no doubt would have caused her severe distress. A diligent and dedicated Nurse would feel tremendous guilt for the loss of a patient in these tragic circumstances. Overlying this there would no doubt have been the terrible knowledge that had she come out into the main body of the ward from the kitchen area at the wrong moment she might have been able to save the girl, although if Griffiths had not been hidden at that point, it seems likely that she may have suffered her fate instead. How could a normal, caring, empathic human being live with the guilt that they could have saved a child's life by sacrificing their own, and, but for a quirk of timing, that is what in fact may have happened? It is sobering to consider what nightmares may have lurked in the unguarded areas of her imagination.

Following her account, evidence was then taken from PC Parkinson and Inspector Wilson who had found the child. They were followed by Albert Devaney, who was a quiet dignified witness.

Dr Gilbert Bailey, a local GP and the police surgeon, was called next. He lived on Preston New Road in Blackburn, which at the time was mainly a leafy highway through the local Beardwood and Fielden estate farmlands. Information about him is scanty, but he appears to have been born in 1890, and to have graduated in medicine from the University of Manchester. He obtained his MRCS and LRCP in 1913, and worked as a Houseman at Manchester, Preston and Southport, before buying into an Insurance Practice in Tottington, Bury. This meant that for a salary he treated patients who were paid up members of the local Workers' Insurance Board. However, it seems that in 1923 he and his partner, a Dr Poole, ended up in serious trouble. It was not uncommon for those receiving treatment from the Board to believe that the medications and interventions were inferior to those given to the fortunate who would pay privately. This was not the case, but they would insist on equivalent private treatments, some even going as far as pouring Board medicines away unused. If this was the case, the doctors were supposed to provide the alternatives free of charge. Instead, it seems that Bailey and Poole had been charging their patients extra for this service. Following an inquiry, it was accepted that they had misunderstood the regulations and had not been deliberately exploiting their clients. Despite agreeing to refund everyone, they were fined £1000 to be repaid from further remuneration. This was a fortune in 1923 and was considered an excessive punishment. A few years later, he moved to Blackburn and became the police surgeon, appearing in court many times to give evidence.

By this time, he had been in medical practice for 34 years, and a police surgeon for 20. Although he had been involved in the Helen Chester case, it was however unlikely that he had seen a murder as repugnant in nature as this. He was first called to give his account of the post mortem examination, detailing as dispassionately as he could the injuries that June had suffered. He was particularly questioned about the significance of the human bite mark on her left buttock, although this did not feature in the forensic evidence. No one had analysed Griffiths' dental work to see if it was a match. Presumably, it was thought not to be necessary given the weight of other evidence.

He stated that the immediate cause of death was a severe head injury, caused by the poor girl being swung by the ankles headfirst against the hospital wall. Mr Neild specifically asked whether the attack had been 'ferocious'. Dr Bailey agreed that it was. Mr Neild then asked, 'In your experience have you ever seen any injuries more consistent than this with the outburst of a lunatic?' Bailey was far too experienced to grandstand for effect, or stray outside of his area of expertise. 'I certainly consider,' he answered dryly, knowing exactly what Neild was asking him to do, 'the man who did this act must have been in a state of maniacal frenzy.' He did not, you notice, confirm that Griffiths had been insane. To make the matter clear, the Judge intervened.

'Does that mean in a condition of complete ferocity?' Yes, the doctor replied. 'A man,' the Judge clarified, 'is not necessarily mad because he acts in a ferocious manner?'

'Not at all,' agreed the doctor.

Seeing a potential line to his defence being closed off, Neild got Bailey to agree that the perpetrator of the crime must have been in a temporary state of mania. He then got Dr Bailey to admit that he had knowledge of schizophrenia, so called *dementia praecox*, commonly misrepresented as a disorder of split personality. Reading this part of the testimony, it is clear that Neild was trying to associate the *concept* of schizophrenia with the *physical presence* of Peter

166

Griffiths in the dock without actually saying straight out that Griffiths was schizophrenic. He managed to get Dr Bailey to suggest that the killer might outwardly seem normal but be subject to episodic sudden episodes of frenzy. The Judge asked if such a person would be certifiable in the medical sense. Dr Bailey asserted that in the normal state, such a man would not be; but that they could be certified as mentally ill during a state of mania if it was severe enough. He concluded eventually, 'If you had an example to work on, my Lord, this is an example now; but previous to this happening, there was probably nothing to work on.' Having been cornered by the Judge in these clarifications, it was then easy for Mr Neild to get Bailey to admit that his first impression on viewing the corpse was that the murderer *must* have been a schizophrenic. However, whilst he agreed that the illness was a defect of the mind, that this did not mean that the killer would always fail to recognise what was right, and what was wrong.

The defence then changed track and turned to general discussion of the characteristics of schizophrenia as a disease, in that there were hereditary elements, and that a typical schizophrenic would have certain personality characteristics, such as social isolation, failure to hold a job, and general apathy. No doubt, on eliciting each characteristic from the doctor, the barrister would have looked significantly towards the accused. Finally, Mr Neild asked, 'Is another matter of great moment, to see whether there is any sort of motive for the crime?'

The doctor replied, 'The motive is simply an uncontrollable sexual impulse. That is all.'

Justice Oliver intervened again at this point, for the Jury's benefit. 'There is a sexual motive here. Whether sane or insane, the jury will decide.'

The prosecution also intervened, asking Bailey to clarify his thoughts. Bailey replied that he had not observed Griffiths, and so could not testify as to his true mentality. 'All I am prepared to say,' he concluded, 'is that the act of murder and rape on this child *could* have been the act of a man with a "split" mind.'

Mr Oliver cross-examined the doctor again, asking if the act could equally have been the act of an extremely ferocious, but not clinically insane, man. The doctor agreed that this could indeed be the case. The man might not have had control over his actions but may well still have known what he was doing. The Judge inquired 'Do you mean that he would know what he was doing, but not know that it was wrong?'

'Whether wrong or not,' replied Dr Bailey, 'he knew what he wanted to do.'

'If he were afterwards to express regret for what he had done, would that, in your view, indicate that he knew what he was doing was wrong when he did it?'

A Court transcript does not record pauses, dramatic intonation, or theatricality. It is, therefore, not clear whether Griffiths knew or understood the implications of the doctor's reply; or whether he imagined the sound of the door of the condemned cell slamming shut behind him, as Dr Bailey replied firmly 'Yes'.

After this dramatic exchange, the trial returned to the mundane procedure of establishing Griffiths' demeanour and movements and confirming his attachment to the evidence.

Thomas Connell was the manager of *Richard Hayes'*
Pawnbrokers, 356 Whalley Road. He confirmed that *exhibit 5*
was a pawn ticket that proved that J Griffiths of Birley Street
had hawked a suit on 31st May 1948, for £1 10s 8d. The "J"
it transpired was not an initial, but apparently indicated that
the person pawning the suit was a male. He identified *exhibit*
6 as the suit that had been taken in, and that it had regularly
been used to secure a five-day loan, usually being pawned on
Monday and redeemed on Friday, payday.

Next up was Rene Edge who confirmed that she was a
weaver and lived at 37 Derby Street. She had known
Griffiths for about 6 years and had started occasionally
'stepping out' with him since Christmas 1947. This
happened more frequently after he was officially
demobilized in February 1948. She also confirmed that the
suit was his. She stated that she met with him on Saturday
16th May, the day after the horrific events at the hospital.
They went for a walk, and the town was all a-buzz with the
talk of the crime. Jokingly, Rene had asked him where he
had been on the Friday night into Saturday morning. He had
said he had gone to town, had a few drinks and gone to bed
about ten forty-five. Chillingly, Griffiths was wearing the
blue suit as he strolled through the town with her.

At one point, marriage had been mentioned. However,
Rene admitted that in mid-April, she had become
disenchanted with his heavy drinking, and had broken up
with him. On 10th May, she accidentally met him in town,
and he had asked her out again. Rene had again turned him
down. The defence asked her, 'That was the last time you
saw him? Until after the death of the child?' It is possible
that it dawned on her at this point that Mr Neild was

suggesting that her refusal to go out with Griffiths was one of the triggers in the death of June. Yes, she had replied. Yes.

Neild continued, 'There was talk of marriage? And four days before this happening you told him you were definitely not changing your mind and going out with him?'

Possibly she paled as she replied, 'That is so.'

Despite their breakup, she confirmed, she continued to occasionally meet with him after the 16th. Griffiths, she confirmed, continued to wear the blue suit on these occasions.

Bernard John Regan was the taxi driver who gave Griffiths a lift to Queens Park. Griffiths had glossed over this in his statement, saying that he had randomly met a stranger driving a car. Regan confirmed that he had picked Griffiths up at Darwen Street Bridge at about ten to midnight, after he had been flagged down; that he had wanted to be taken to Queen's Park, near the entrance to the Delph across the clay pit, for five shillings; and that after he had left him he had watched him head off towards the quarry. He indicated Griffiths' movements on a series of photographs coded as *exhibit 1*. Regan stated that he had gone to the police the week after the murder to tell them of the man in the blue suit who had wanted to go to the hospital on the night of the murder, and how on 25th August he had unhesitatingly picked Griffiths out of an identification parade. At this point, Mr Neild pounced, and tried to imply that his evidence was contaminated.

'Is it right to say that you had carried many people (in your cab) during that three and a half months (between the murder and the parade)?'

'Yes.'

'Is it also right to say that before you attended that identification parade you had seen a photograph of this accused man in the newspapers?'

'I had.'

'Did you, before the parade say, "I am not sure I can pick out the man"?'

'I did.'

'Did you say that just before the parade, or at the parade?'

'Just as I got into the room to identify him.'

'When certain men were standing there?'

'Yes, in front of me.'

'When you were asked to point to the man, did you touch the accused?'

'I walked up to him and touched him.'

'Did you say "I am almost sure this is the man"?'

'Yes'

At the cross examination by the prosecution, Regan identified Griffiths as the man he had identified in the line-up, and the man that he had driven up to the Park. The discrepancies between Griffiths' statement and Regan's were not explored at this stage.

Other witnesses came and went in a flurry. PC Joseph Calvert confirmed that on 11th August he had taken Griffith's fingerprints at his home in Birley Street. They were immortalised as *Exhibit 7*. Capstick gave evidence surrounding the arrest. He was very careful to say that Griffiths had been cautioned by Barton when arrested, once again in the back of the car on the way to the station, and then again on arrival. There was no way that Griffiths could not have known or understood that he was a suspect in the child's murder, or that anything he said would be used in Court. Capstick admitted that he had been left alone with the prisoner twice, and that he took the statement of guilt, *Exhibit 8*, in the presence of Inspector Barton, and Detective Sergeant Mullen. He confirmed that the identity parade was established according to the Home Office Rules. He also said that on 26th August they had approached Griffiths to provide samples such as pubic hair. He had declined, saying 'I would not care to.'

Regan and Capstick's evidence was supplemented by John Alfred Dennett, the Deputy Governor of Walton Jail, save that he believed that Regan had said only 'I am almost sure that is the man' rather than expressing any previous uncertainty about identifying him. Detective Sergeant Mullen detailed how he had found the pawn ticket at the Birley Street address, and a blue sock, *exhibit 25*, containing a red stripe which matched the threads found on the footprints in the ward. He also confirmed that he himself had walked the path from the gap in the hospital fence to the Delph, and that it could be run in three minutes. The path and the fence were easily negotiable.

Inspector Bill Barton confirmed his role in arresting the accused, and taking a second set of prints, *exhibit 10*, which were found not useful due to the excessive sweating of the prisoner. These were therefore later repeated and re-entered as *exhibit 14*. He also took evidential footprints of Griffiths in his stockinged feet, and a full palm print. These exhibits, *11, 12* and *13*, were all forwarded to Hutton, where they were found to match those found at the scene.

Barton also stated that he knew Griffiths' father well. He was a loom sweeper in a cotton factory, the least skilled form of work. He was also familiar with his medical history. Following his head injury, a bullet or shrapnel wound to the forehead received in the trenches, he was an in-patient in

Prestwich County Mental Hospital between July 1918 and March 1919. He had been classified as recovered but could only hold down low-end jobs. Barton had first encountered Griffiths senior in 1931 when he had suffered a hallucinogenic episode. He claimed to have seen four men wanted for a murder in Yorkshire driving through Blackburn in the early hours. The report was completely unfounded.

Mr Neild elicited evidence from Barton to show that Peter Griffiths came from a very poor and disadvantaged background. He then confirmed that Griffiths himself had been hospitalised from February 1936 to February 1938, and that when he was old enough to be employed, he had just drifted episodically from one dead end job to another, until he was drafted into the Army on 17th February 1944. He was slightly wounded in Northern Europe but was generally unstable in army life. He had deserted twice, and was regarded as an indifferent, bad soldier. There was however no evidence of mental instability in his record, and Barton had been unable to find any records that Griffiths himself had ever been treated for mental illness.

At the time of the murder, he had worked on and off in the flour mill until 21st May. This was the only job he had acquired since the Army.

Detective Inspector Campbell was asked to talk the Jury around his examination of the crime scene and all the evidence that he had gathered. In particular, he had to describe how Nurse Humphreys had drawn his attention to the sterile water bottle, and how he had lifted the tell-tale fingerprints and palm print of the killer from it. The bottle was *exhibit 4*. The prints were *exhibits 13* and *14*. They matched Griffiths' fingerprints taken by the police during the manhunt. Photographic enlargements, *exhibits 18 -22*,

173

were used to illustrate to the jury the similarities between the prints. Campbell concluded firmly, 'I have no doubt whatever that the imprints to which I have referred on the bottle were made by the same person who signed the form "Peter Griffiths".'

He also described how he had isolated and lifted the footprints and the threads from blue grey socks with a red pattern in them that had been found. These were labelled *A.15/5/48/CMC, B15/5/48/CMC* and *G15/5/48/CMC*. The left and right footprints were not alike but had characteristic abnormalities, and Campbell described how they matched footprints that Griffiths had provided whilst in custody. The evidence was firmed up further when Home Office Forensic Science Biologist David Noel Jones matched fibres found to the socks and suit that were retrieved from Griffiths. He also analysed hair and blood from the stone wall and matched it to June Anne. This meant that her head had contacted the wall with force several times. He confirmed that her blood group was type A. The blue suit that Griffiths had tried to conceal in the pawn shop matched fibres found on the scene and the child and was spattered with spots of blood group A on the crotch and legs, pockets, lapels and sleeves.

The Jury were allowed to contemplate this dreadful information for a few seconds, before Gorman turned to the Courtroom and announced that the Prosecution rested. What could the defence do against such a mountain of evidence?

The defence of course was not trying to prove that Griffiths was innocent but to show that he did not deserve the death penalty. The grounds for the defence was that when he abducted and killed the girl, he was not in his right mind so that he did not know what he was doing was wrong. Neild summarised the defence concisely in one phrase in his long opening speech. 'You may be quite satisfied,' he announced , 'that on Saturday 15th May, this little child June Anne Devaney , only three years of age, was snatched from her cot, taken into a field below this hospital, wickedly assaulted and ravished in circumstances that caused us all anguish of mind, and then battered to death against a wall. Upon these bare, perhaps brutal, recounting of these facts I ask you, as ordinary citizens, whether each of you does not think this at once: that the man who did these things *must* have been mad. *That* is the case which I have to present to you: that *this* man, at *that* time, *was* mad.'

To support the findings of insanity, he would ask the Jury to consider the family history, the accused's personal medical history, the impression of Dr Bailey that the killer was in a frenzy, the facts that Griffiths had been subjected to some stressful circumstances which may have triggered the attack, and his return to normality despite committing a heinous act. What were these stressors? On 8th May Griffiths witnessed a terrible argument between his brother and his estranged wife. Mrs Brennan had moved out some time ago, taking her children, the nieces and nephews so beloved by Griffiths, with her. The argument had been triggered by the news that young Pauline Brennan, one of Griffiths' favourites, had been admitted to hospital and that if Mrs Brennan had her way neither Brennan, nor the Griffiths', would see her again. Pauline Brennan was at that time an inpatient in the toddler's section of ward CH3. On the 10th May, Rene Edge jilted him. On 14th May, these traumatic events whirled around in Griffiths head when he went on his enormous pub crawl. Perhaps, in his befuddled state Griffiths wished to check on the well-being of his niece? Who can say? He certainly did not go there with the intent of killing the girl. But, when he got to the ward, the ward where he had spent so much of his youth, something undefinable, something unthinkable, something unknown even to Griffiths himself, dispossessed him of his reason and he then engaged upon his unspeakable act

As the first day of the trial ended, Neild turned to the Jury, looked them in the eye, and said 'I am not asking for this man's liberty, but I shall ask you to say upon the evidence, when you have heard it, that it is not merely humane or merciful, but it is right and just that you should say "Guilty of the act, but insane at the time".'

Chapter 25

The Second Day

Lancaster
18th October 1968

The Jury, and Griffiths, had all of the weekend to contemplate the case that had been made by the prosecution.

Monday 18th October opened with Mrs Elizabeth Alice Griffiths, mother of the accused, being called to give evidence. She confirmed the complex family history and social arrangements, and the facts relating to her husband's mental illness, of which she was unaware when she had married him on 28th June 1923. She concurred with Inspector Barton regarding her husband's psychotic episode in 1931, and confirmed details of Peter Griffiths' medical history, particularly a near fatal head injury he had suffered aged 6, and the later long-term incarceration in hospital.

She confirmed to the Court that her son's wardrobe was very limited. He really only possessed his khaki uniform, which he was wearing in the dock, and the blue suit, which she had brought to the pawnbrokers for him

Unaware of what time he had arrived home on the night of the murder, the next morning she had asked him what he had been up to, and he had lied to her. He behaved normally as far as she was concerned right up to the time of his arrest. It was a shock, a great shock, to find out what he had done. He had always been strange, a loner, playing trains with matchboxes for hours. She had always told him to stop it, because people would think he was 'mental'.

James Brennan, the stepbrother, confirmed that Griffiths had witnessed a row between him and his estranged wife, in which she revealed young Pauline was in the hospital, and that she had threatened Brennan with never seeing his children again. The morning after the murder, he recalled, his half-brother's blue suit had been hanging on the door, waiting to be pressed, and Griffiths had been wearing his khakis.

Elizabeth Ellen Brennan was the estranged wife of James, and confirmed the version of events that had been given. She described how Griffiths loved children, doted on them, played with them. 'He loved children, thought a lot about children...He was a queer boy, and was not like a normal lad of his age because he never had any friends or pals to go out with- he was always alone, even as a small child he was like that.'

Having set the background, the defence then wheeled out its big gun. Dr Alastair Robertson Grant, JP, Psychiatrist at the Whittingham Hospital, near Preston, for 17 years. Grant was a distinguished psychiatrist, becoming a member of the Association of Psychiatrists in 1921 when he was Assistant Medical Officer at Whittingham. He eventually became head of the Hospital. He received an OBE and died in 1986. Whittingham was one of a string of Lancashire Mental Asylums Founded in 1873. By 1939 it was self-sufficient complex housing 3500 patients, and over 500 staff, the largest facility of its type in Europe, with its own railway station. Amongst other things, it was a European centre of excellence for the treatment of the incurable neurological illness Huntington's disease. However, Whittingham would later be the source of much controversy. Between 1967 and 1968, nursing students complained repeatedly about the way the patients were being treated. The complaints were ignored, and the nurses silenced by threats and indifference. With the support of a new psychologist, the complaints re-emerged and in 1971 a public enquiry upheld the nurses' issues. In addition, the authorities found evidence of poor facilities, financial mismanagement and fraud. Eventually, a nurse was convicted of manslaughter. Changes were made, but the hospital was mired in trouble again in the 1990's. Staff were convicted of having sex with patients and a patient who was discharged went on to commit a murder. The hospital finally closed in ignominy in 1995. But that was all in the future. Grant was now being asked to give his expert opinion on Griffiths' mind. Neild was confident. Events were not to unfold as he expected, however.

Grant had examined Griffiths twice, on 28th September and 8th October. He admitted that during the examinations, Griffiths had given him an account of what had happened in the early hours of the 15th May, and Neild asked him to elaborate on his findings.

God loves a tryer, but Justice Oliver intervened. 'I do not for the moment see how a statement *not* on oath to a doctor about the facts of the case can be admissible, when there is available a witness who *can* give evidence on oath [to the court] ...I do not think you can ask him to give a statement in narrative form of what this man told him happened that night. It is nothing but hearsay, and not admissible on any principle of law.'

Neild at this point offered to provide justification as to why allowing Grant's full reasoning about Griffiths would not be incorrect, when the Judge interrupted, describing it as 'improper'. Neild protested, but Justice Oliver retorted sharply, 'I do not think that is right.' The prosecution unsurprisingly sided with the Judge. Neild argued desperately that the full consultation with Griffiths might reveal the sort of symptoms or delusions that Griffiths suffered from and might confirm a diagnosis. The Judge was firm. 'Patchy recollection...if a man has too much to drink, his memory might be hazy. I do not think it is admissible, and I rule against it.'

The Judge was certainly correct in that if this sort of evidence about the crime was to be heard, it should come from Griffiths himself, not through a third party. The last thing that Neild would have wanted of course was to have the prisoner at the bar in the stand describing in detail how he abducted and murdered a child, but he desperately needed Grant's unexpurgated evidence. No matter how correct the Judge's ruling was, the net result was that the heart of the medical defence had been ripped out.

The exact details of what this defence would have revealed remain shrouded in darkness, as later applications to make this evidence available for the Appeal, and then a textbook about the trial, were turned down. It has been asserted in fact that Grant later privately admitted that having considered Griffith's account over time that he was probably of sound mind. But that was not the nature of his evidence at the trial.

When the trial was over, many of the medical profession vented their outrage on what they saw as an attack on their integrity, and a debate raged throughout the medical world. Surely, the Court was straying beyond its fields of expertise? Surely it was for doctors to determine what evidence was required to make a diagnosis on the mental state of any patient, not a Court or a Judge who were, after all, *only laymen*, no matter how prestigious they were? Surely, only the medical profession could determine whether an individual was suffering from a disease of the mind? And to determine whether they were responsible for their actions at the time of the crime? In addition, as resources available to the State are effectively limitless, and those to the defence, particularly in the case of a financially challenged individual such as Griffiths, were not, it was felt that the prosecution had the advantage in locating and commissioning experts. The expert, of course, was providing neutral evidence to the Court, but there was always a suspicion that they had one eye on the man paying the piper.

For example, on November 13th 1948, the *British Medical Journal* published an editorial dealing with the Griffiths case and the M'Naghten rules. An outline of the facts of the crime was followed by a brief description of Griffiths' mental history, and then a discussion of the M'Naghten case. The article concluded that although there were doubts about his sanity, that because there were aspects of his actions that showed that Griffiths knew what he was doing was wrong and that there was no defence in British Law of succumbing to an irresistible impulse, he was not insane under the law. The article finished by saying

> '..this is a typical borderline case of the kind which raises again the question of whether the M'Naghten rules, so clearly anachronistic and out of line with modern knowledge of the mind and of responsibility ought any longer to be tolerated. Their amazing persistence is due to several factors...they work unexpectedly well...[and]..the Home Secretary's exercise of the Royal Prerogative [to commute the sentence to life] stands behind the court to prevent a miscarriage of Justice...'

The following fortnight the journal published a letter from a Dr Clifford Allen, who did not feel that doctors employed by the prison services should be able to give an opinion on a convict's state of mind, as they were not experts. He wrote: 'There has been case after case in which the murderer has been stated by a competent psychiatrist to be insane, but on the opinion of a prison doctor (who is usually a general practitioner without psychiatric experience) the issue has been placed in doubt. The M'Naghten rules have been produced and the prisoner found guilty...if a patient came to one and stated that his father had been insane and he himself had impulses to murder children would any psychiatrist hesitate to certify him? Of course not. Yet, if he does the murder and is seen afterwards he is found guilty of malice aforethought and hanged...It is time that psychiatrists stood out against the anachronism of the law...'

Replies in December were not all in favour of his view, citing the fairness and wisdom of Judges in ensuring that all views were properly contextualised. The last word was given to a Dr Packenham Walsh, who reflected that in the 1920s, attempted suicides were nursed to recovery with a police officer in the ward ready to arrest them for the crime as soon as they were recovered. His letter finished '...perhaps in a further twenty years' time all those who have proved themselves to be a danger to others will be allowed to live peacefully under supervision in the hospitals provided for that purpose, instead of being prematurely dispatched to another world...'

Perhaps if Grant's evidence had been admitted, it would have confirmed that Griffiths had a clear mental health diagnosis. Perhaps it would have revealed what it was that triggered Griffiths to commit such a monstrous act, what it was that had turned him from Peter the shy introvert loner man-child, into Griffiths the monster. Was it a fluke of aberrant biochemistry, or had he finally lost control of the Demon that had always dwelt within him? Perhaps an opportunity to learn and prevent another such occurrence was missed by the Judge's ruling, no matter how legally precise it was. In the end, the medical controversy came to naught.

Neild had to cope with the hand he had been dealt, and so he soldiered on. When prompted, Grant had no hesitation in diagnosing Griffiths with 'early schizophrenia'. When the doctor justified this by mentioning Griffiths' father's own mental health incarceration, the Judge interrupted again. He made it clear that the doctor had not seen the medical records of Griffiths' senior, and only knew this information from second-hand sources. This gave the impression that the doctor was prone to making assumptions that affected his evidence. Neild had to reword his line of questioning, starting with the words 'Assuming this man's father was admitted...'

Grant then explained that he had been told that Griffiths' senior had been an inpatient at Prestwich asylum from 20th July 1918, with delusional insanity. Justice Oliver used the phrase 'dangerous lunatic soldier,' the official term used at the time. Grant confirmed that Griffiths' father would have been diagnosed as schizophrenic had the term existed at the time, and that in 60% of cases there was evidence of hereditary predisposition. It would not have been caused by his head wound, but by an inbuilt, inherited disorder. One might inherit the tendency, but not display the symptoms until a moment of stress triggered abnormal reactions in the brain, and the breakdown surfaced. The Judge interrupted again when the witness gave evidence about Griffiths junior's two-year admission to CH3, aged 8. Again, Dr Grant had not seen the records for himself. He had to admit that he had been told this by the instructing solicitor. Again, Neild had to start his questions with the word 'assuming'. Dr Grant confirmed that incontinence of urine, the stated cause of the two years in-patient admission, was often a sign of neurosis, which was often a precursor of schizophrenia. Such a neurotic, pre-schizophrenic person would have a solitary, childish personality. Again, Justice Oliver intervened. What was the time scale of onset of schizophrenia? It could be years, or it could be very sudden. In fact, you could not really predict how long it took to present. Griffiths' personality, his work record, his poor performance in the army, all supported a diagnosis of paranoid schizophrenia. Excess drink coupled with the breakdown of his relationship with Miss Edge could all trigger a schizophrenic episode. He too confirmed that the killer of June Anne Devaney was in a frenzy at the time the murder occurred. The bite on her buttock confirmed it. 'You mean,' Justice Oliver interrupted, 'as I understand it, the rape itself and the brutality accompanying it, was the work of a maniac?'

'In my opinion,' the doctor replied, 'yes.'

Grant added that the murder was part of the same maniacal act. He also confirmed that the fact that Griffiths was able to return home, behave normally in front of his family, and Rene , and even pursue his relationship with her; and even the fact that he could remain calm when the police called to take his brother's fingerprints, and again when they returned to take his own; the fact that he could remain impassive and un-empathic when the whole town was talking about the killing, and it was in every newspaper in the land; all pointed to a firm diagnosis of schizophrenia. The fact that he expressed regret in his confession was not inconsistent with the condition. In response to Neild's final question, about what may have been going through Griffiths' mind at the exact time of the murder, Grant responded 'I think he *knew* what he was doing, but I do not think he *fully appreciated* he was doing wrong.'

One might think, reading the transcript of the trial, that Grant had already been cross examined by the Judge as he was giving his evidence, but now he faced the official interrogation from the prosecution. One can almost hear the *faux* astonishment in Gorman's voice as he launched a series of attacks on Grant's thoroughness. For example, he got

Grant to admit that when treating a member of the public unfortunate enough to be admitted to a mental hospital, that it may take daily observation for several weeks to reach a diagnosis and treatment plan. And yet, he was able to make a diagnosis after seeing Griffiths for a total of only *two hours?* Incredible!

Gorman then changed tack. He wanted specifics. He wanted Grant to give the exact *time* on the night of 14th /15th May that Griffiths had crossed the line from normality into insanity.

'At the time he was violating the child or trying to kill it,' Grant replied

'The mania developed when he was attacking the child?'

'I think so.'

'At what stage did it cease?'

'After he had killed the child.'

That seemed straightforward enough, but Gorman pressed him further. At what stage did the madness cease *exactly?* An unspecified time after the child had been killed. So up until the attack commenced, and after it finished this man was his normal self? Yes, apart from the alcohol. Would he not have suffered a memory lapse- a blank- during the attack? Not necessarily. In some cases, the schizophrenic had total recall of the violent attacks they had perpetrated.

'You heard the man's statement read out in court, doctor? Did you notice the discrepancy between his account of how he got to Queens Park hospital and the account of Mr Regan? If Mr Regan's evidence is true, then his version is not true. Does that not seem to you that this is the *conscious* effort of a man to cover his tracks by saying it was an unknown person rather than a Taxi driver who might be traced?'

186

If Grant may have hesitated before giving his answer, sensing a trap, the transcript does not reveal. 'That is quite possible.'

Now Gorman had a way in, a chink in the armour, and the questions came thick and fast. Leaving his shoes outside the door of the ward: that is an obviously stealthy act? Quite. And the mind of this man would know what it was that was causing him to act stealthily? I take it so, yes. Hiding from the nurse, leaving the ward when she entered and then returning, this is the action of a man who knew he was doing wrong? He knew what he was doing at that time, yes. A man so mentally alert, he was awaiting until the coast was clear? Yes. Picking a bottle off the shelf, did it occur to you that this was to prevent surprise? No, I must say it did not. The fact that when arrested he volunteered to the officers that they might be coming to him because it was his fingerprints on the bottle, that he remembered enough to associate this with his arrest, this is a mind working normally and perfectly? Yes. Are his actions not those of a man who was conscious that he was doing something he should not be doing? Yes. You know the footprints show that he went to three cots? He would know what he was doing then? Yes, allowed the doctor.

The line of questioning continued, and as it did, Grant was undermining his own conclusions, painting a clearer and clearer picture that Griffiths was in his right mind when he abducted young June; that he knew exactly what he was doing when he walked up and down the ward; that he entered the ward with the specific intention of taking a child, with murder in his heart. And that, when he did so, he was not insane, not mad, not in the grip of a maniacal frenzy. Just all too human. The skilful questioning which pulled increasingly monosyballic answers from Dr Grant painted a transparent picture. Griffiths was a monster after all. Bad, then, not mad.

The prosecution then used Dr Grant to dissect Griffiths' police statement. This basically repeated all that had gone before, but the specific purpose was, of course, to remind the Jury of the horrible crime with words from the perpetrator's own mouth. The passage where June was taken was dwelt upon with particular relish.

'..."I picked the girl up out of the cot and took her outside by the same door. I carried her in my right arm, and she put her arms around my neck and I walked with her down the hospital field"- [was he] perfectly normal to that point?'

'Yes.'

' "I put her down on the grass" Was the mind normal up to that point?'

'I should not have thought so, no.'

Again, the Barrister pounced. 'Where did he cease to be normal?'

The question of course is impossible for a professional to answer with any certainty. It is likely that Griffiths was never actually normal in his life, just contained. But Grant was obliged to try and explain, and the legitimate uncertainties made him look vacillating and weak. 'It is very difficult to say,' he floundered, 'but I should say after he took the child out of the cot.'

But the prosecutor wanted to pin him down precisely. When he put her on the grass, was that not the conscious act of a man who wanted to assault that child? The doctor disagreed: the schizoid attack could have started when he picked the child up in the cot, but the mania not manifest until he started to attack her.

'…"and you know what happened then.",' Gorman quoted Griffiths' only description of the crime, and one can almost hear the theatrical weight given to those six deadly words, 'is that not the statement of a man who is saying, "I know what I did; and you know what I did; but it is too horrible for me to mention."?'

Dr Grant conceded it was a difficult point. He knew of other cases where men had committed similar horrid acts, and who's memory of events was good, but who were proven to be insane. By that statement, it was not clear to the doctor whether Griffiths meant that the police knew exactly what he had done, but he himself had no recollection. Maybe he recalled he had taken a child, but not the murder. Perhaps he recalled the murder, but not the assault. It was not clear.

There then followed a discussion about the syntax of the confession itself. Was there a full stop between the words 'you know what happened then' and 'I banged her head against the wall'? If there was a comma instead, the whole context changed from a blurred description of two events, to one ('You know what happened then, I banged her head against the wall.') in which no suggestion of assault occurred. In any event, according to Dr Grant all possible interpretations were consistent with a diagnosis of schizophrenia. If Griffiths did not recall the assault, the partial amnesia could be alcohol induced. A schizophrenic would either remember all, or none, not some.

'Are you suggesting, that the sanity of this man returned at the point represented by the word "wall" in that statement?' The doctor had to reply that it was difficult to say.

'Do you think that he ever came to the realisation that he was doing wrong?'

'Yes,' mused the doctor, 'but his mental responses are very blunted about the whole thing afterwards.... not at the time that he did it. He realised afterwards.'

Questioning then turned to Griffiths' actions and statements in the days after the murder. When he lied to Rene Edge and his mother about his actions, when he expressed remorse in his statement, these were all signs of guilt, of knowledge that he had done wrong? Remorse, said the doctor, was not an alien concept to people with mental health issues.

'Will you tell me what there is in his statement that enables you to take a portion of time and say that within that portion of time this man was in this mental state?' All aspects of the attack indicated it. 'But where do you draw the line?' At the time that the child was killed, because of his clear recollection prior to and after the event.

The Judge then intervened again. Why, then, if he was in his right mind, and did not have murderous intent, until he started the attack, did Griffiths take the child from the hospital to the field?

There was a pause, and the doctor there had to admit the limit of his reasoning. 'I...have no idea.'

The schizophrenic mania did not exist at the time he took the child from her cot, clarified Justice Oliver, because he would have bashed her brains out there and then? Yes.

The prosecution then went in for the kill. Look at the man in the dock, as he is now. You would not consider his father's history to be of any relevance in his current condition, would you? Even if you did, his father had not had treatment for over thirty years. The family, the girlfriend, were shocked when he was arrested. They clearly did not expect madness. Because the truth was that he was not, and never had been, *at any time*, mad.

The defence tried to salvage the situation, but it was no good, the damage was done. The family history was relevant, it was argued. Griffiths had inherited the taint, and on the night in question, at some point, it was irrelevant exactly when, he began to lose control of his actions. He took the child, no one knew why, he did not know why; he was overtaken with a maniacal murderous frenzy because she was crying, the details of which he did not fully remember; and then, slowly, he began to return to normal, developing as he did a sense , however limited, of remorse. Are there other cases in your experience like this? He asked Grant, rather weakly

Yes, replied Dr Grant, rather pointedly, in a case of murder tried at Liverpool before Justice Oliver, where Mr Nield was again the defence attorney.

'I want,' the Judge said, before Grant left the stand, 'to ask you one thing. Do you regard the raping of even small children as evidence of insanity?'

Did Grant feel a heavy weight in his heart as he answered honestly? 'No.'

'There have been millions of cases where men have been convicted of such crimes, guilty of lust but not insanity?' Yes.

The child must have suffered greatly during the attack. Is there anything mad, in the child screaming because of the brutality she was suffering, in the fact that he beat her head against the wall? Surely, he only did it to silence her so he could escape?

On this point, the doctor disagreed. Griffiths had no reason to kill her, a child as young as that could not have given evidence against him. He killed her only because he was mad, at that time.

After his dismissal, the Court called another psychiatrist, Dr Geoffrey Talbot, Medical Superintendent of Prestwich Mental Hospital, Manchester. He confirmed that Peter Griffiths Sr. had been admitted in 1918 suffering from paranoid schizophrenia. He had not examined Griffiths Jr., but he had listened to the evidence given by Dr Grant and agreed with his opinion.

And that concluded the case for the defence.

The prosecution called its own expert in rebuttal. Dr Francis Herbert Brisby, Principal Medical Officer at HMP Liverpool, previously an Assistant Medical Officer at a Lancaster County Mental Hospital. Brisby's evidence was particularly cogent because whilst incarcerated Griffiths was under his care and he had the medical opportunity to observe the accused over a long period of time, longer than Grant, longer than Talbot, who had not seen him at all. He stated to the Court that a schizophrenic would have had no recollection of such a crime. He stated very clearly that from his detailed observations, he found no evidence of any disease of the mind that would prevent Griffiths from either knowing what he was doing, or that it was wrong. Neild took him slowly through all the symptoms of schizophrenia that Grant had identified in Griffiths. Brisby agreed they were all symptoms of serious mental illness. He even agreed that Griffiths Sr. probably did have paranoid schizophrenia.

However, he remained of the opinion that he had identified no mental illness in Griffiths the killer.

Surely, postulated the defence, your opinion relates only to the dates that Griffiths was under your care? No, from his description of events, his opinion covered the period of the murder also. There was no cogent evidence that Griffiths had schizophrenia himself. No evidence at all.

So, that was the case. The defence argued using its experts that Griffiths was insane at the time of the murder; the prosecution's expert said that he was not. The defence concentrated on family history, symptoms and a history of trauma; the prosecution concentrated on tying the defence in knots by arguing about when the insanity started and ended, as if it could be flicked on and off like a switch. The Jury had time to mull this over whilst the barristers espoused their closing speeches.

Mr Neild outlined that he was not allowed to make admissions on behalf of his client, Peter Griffiths who had chosen not to give evidence himself. Neither were the Jury to derive any intimation from this. The sole defence case was that Griffiths was insane, in the legal sense, when committed the crime. Griffiths was a schizophrenic, outwardly normal but suffering from a terrible mental affliction, a defect of the mind that was triggered on 14th May with murderous results. It can be no coincidence that the set of fingerprints that identified the murderer identified a man whose father also suffered from schizophrenia, who had suffered a precipitating head injury as a child, who had spent two years in hospital as an adolescent with a neurotic disorder, who had a strange and solitary personality, who played as a child when he was an adult. The medical witnesses all agreed on the signs and symptoms displayed by

Griffiths but disagreed only in how they interpreted them. The crime was indeed hideous, but a Court is not the place for vengeance, but justice. It was just to conclude that Griffiths was insane. 'Do not think,' he said, 'in years to come that I hope my decision was right; know that it was right'. His final closing words were those he had used at the start: 'Let your verdict be "guilty of the act, but insane at the time".'

Mr Gorman refuted everything that Mr Neild had said. Do not, he said, conclude that just because the crime was unspeakable in nature that the perpetrator must have been insane. Whatever the man's family and personal history, the division of the opinions of the doctors meant that the case for schizophrenia was not proven. After all, even Dr Grant could not identify the exact point that the madness took over. Do not forget, this is a man who took off his shoes to stealthily enter a hospital ward, to steal a child, to conceal his acts by taking her a distance away, who did what he could to conceal the act, who lied to his friends and family, who, most importantly, knew what he was doing was wrong. Despite all the suggestion of madness, he was passed fit to serve his country. The failure to run after the crime was not the befuddled actions of a confused psychopath; it was the conscious act of a sane man, who hoped to conceal his guilt by staying hidden in the crowd; a man who failed to appreciate that a dogged and determined policeman would fingerprint over 46,000 individuals to track him down. Griffiths was not insane then, he was not insane now, he was never insane. He was driven by unnatural lust, and was guilty of the most hideous, premeditated murder.

The last words went to Justice Oliver, who briefly reminded everyone that this was a 'most dreadful' case. It was truly a ferocious, shocking crime, and there was no doubt that Griffiths was indeed guilty of it. The evidence suggests it, and the confession seals it. The sole question before them was the man's state of mind. He re-iterated the evidence in all its detail. Having potential for schizophrenia, is not the same as being schizophrenic; and being schizophrenic is not the same as being insane at the very moment the crime occurred. He succinctly outlined the decision the Jury had to make. 'When this man did this act-I am assuming he did it- when he did this act, did he know that what he was doing was wrong? And if he did, then your verdict must be "Guilty-of murder".'

Chapter 26

Verdict

Lancaster
18th October 1948

A t 4:40pm, the Judge dismissed the jury to consider their verdict, and they filed out to digest all they had told. It is always uncertain how long these deliberations would take. Sometimes it would be days, and they would have to be housed in local hotels, banned from discussing the case with family, reading about it in the paper, or listening to news about it on the wireless. The lawyers and witnesses never knew what to do at this point. Step out home? Stay? Return to other work? The local and national press reporters planned headlines that might not be required for some time.

As it was, they barely had time to seek out a cup of tea.

The Judge reconvened the Court at five past five. The Jury shuffled in and took their places. The gallery bristled with excitement as the room hushed to allow justice to take its course.

The clerk of the court asked the Jury to confirm if they had elected a foreman to speak for them. The foreman stood, and was asked if they had reached a verdict on which they were all agreed? The foreman confirmed that they had.

'Members of the Jury,' the Clerk intoned, 'do you find Peter Griffiths guilty? Or not guilty?'

The foreman said, clearly, and without doubt, 'Guilty.'

'That is the verdict of you all?'

'Yes.'

The Clerk turned to the pale faced man in the Dock who seemed somewhat indifferent to the verdict and the murmurings of the witnesses and audience. 'Peter Griffiths,' he intoned, 'you have been convicted of murder upon the verdict of the Jury. Have you anything to say why the Court should not pass sentence of death upon you, according to the law?'

Griffiths looked up, perhaps startled at being addressed directly, and perhaps puzzled, apparently emotionless. He shook his head slightly. 'No.'

The Clerk then turned to the whole room, demanding that they keep silent whilst sentence of death was passed upon the prisoner. The sentence for breaking the silence would be imprisonment.

Justice Oliver donned the traditional black cap, and said 'Peter Griffiths, this jury has found you guilty of a crime of the most brutal ferocity. I entirely agree with their verdict. The sentence of the Court upon you is that you be taken from this place to a lawful prison; and thence to a place of execution; and that there you suffer death by hanging. And that your body afterwards be buried within the precincts of the prison in which you have been confined before your execution. And may the Lord have mercy on your soul.'

The very last word went to the Court Chaplain, there to provide comfort and solace to the condemned. 'Amen,' he murmured. 'Amen.'

Chapter 27

The 8 o 'clock Walk

HMP Liverpool
19th November 1948

Peter Griffiths was executed on 19th November 1948 by Harry Bernard Allen, who had the distinction of being one of the two people to be Britain's last executioners.

Allen was born in 1911 in Yorkshire. After leaving school, he joined the local corporation bus company, where he was a driver. Like his executioner colleagues, he led a strange double life, continuing this every-day trade long after becoming a hangman. He became an executioner in the usual way, by application to the Home Office, and was assistant first to Tom Pierrepoint, and then his more famous nephew, Albert. He first witnessed an execution at the age of

29, that of William Cooper in 1940. Cooper was a farmhand who had been dismissed for disobedience by farmer John Harrison. Knowing that Harrison would be dealing with the cash payroll in an isolated farm building on a Friday, Cooper attempted to rob him, and accidentally battered him to death with a bottle of *Tizer*. Sadly, that week, Harrison had broken the habit of a lifetime and paid the labourers on a Thursday, so Cooper had only escaped with a tiny amount of cash. Having found out that he was not too squeamish for the job, despite the fact that Cooper had to be carried to the scaffold in a dead faint, Allen became a fully trained hangman, fitting the work in around his driving job, and later his role as a publican, first in Farnworth, and later in Whitefield. He acted as an assistant on many executions, including War Criminals, and eventually became joint Chief Executioner. During his career he helped to hang, amongst others, the wrongly convicted Timothy Evans and later the true culprit John Christie; and Derek Bentley. He also executed the mad-dog family killer Peter Manuel, whose last words when the secret door to the condemned cell swung open were reputedly 'Turn up the radio, boys, and I'll come quietly'. It was during this execution that Allen's first wife left him. He was also responsible for carrying out the legal penalty on Gunther Podola, the last man executed in Britain for the murder of a policeman, Detective Sergeant Ray Purdy, during an attempt to blackmail the model Verne Schiffman for the return of the jewellery and furs he had stolen from her; and the notorious A6 killer, James Hanratty in 1962 for the murder of Michael Gregsten and the abduction, rape and attempted murder of his lover Valerie Storie, who was left paralysed. Hanratty's family continued to campaign for his conviction to be quashed until 2002 when DNA from his exhumed body was found to be an exact match to that found at the murder scene. Allen, meantime, had never had any qualms about Hanratty's fate. He also presided over the executions of EOKA terrorists in Cyprus, over the last hanging in Northern Ireland, Robert McGladdery killer of Pearle Gamble; and the last judicial hanging in Scotland, Henry Burnett, for the shotgun murder of Thomas Guyan, the husband of his paramour. Allen's final ever execution was that of Gwyne Owen Evans on 13th August 1964 at the same time as his colleague Robert Stewart executed Evans' partner in crime, Peter Anthony Allen, at a different prison. These two men were the last ever to be executed in the UK.

Henry Allen always took his duties seriously and insisted on wearing a bowler hat and a black bow tie as a sign of respect to the condemned. After the death penalty was abolished, he retired, eventually moving to Fleetwood in 1977 where he worked as a cashier on the pier. He died in 1992, one month after his mentor, Albert Pierrepoint, and after his death some of his bow ties were auctioned for charity.

Some years later, it became apparent that Allen had kept a diary of every execution he had been involved with. In it, he made a record of the date, the name, age, height and, crucially, the length of drop used to end the lives of his customers. A sort of self-audit, if you will, with extra comments of interest. His entry in relation to Peter Griffiths reads:

Peter Griffiths
Age: 22 years
Height: 5' 10"
Weight: 148 lbs
Drop: 7'6"

James Watts & Thomas Watts

Remarks:
Very good job at Walton Prison, Liverpool. Time 30 seconds
[from entering the condemned cell, until death]. *Blackburn
child murderer. Mrs Violet van der Elst was at the Prison gate. This
was the second execution since the abolition.*

The presiding executioner, Albert Pierrepoint, said in an
interview that Griffiths had died 'like a soldier' presumably
meaning that he went calmly and obediently to the noose.

As mentioned, Violet van der Elst and her crew stood
vigil outside. Perhaps, as he took the last walk he would ever
take, Griffiths heard their hymns wafting through the
corridors after him, like the sound of sea through a shell.

That, then was the bad end faced by the eerie young man
who became, albeit however briefly, infamous as the worst
kind of monster. Opinion was divided as to whether his
destiny, and that of his distressingly innocent victim, was
predetermined by genetics, health, circumstances or drink;
and medical examination could not determine if he was
permanently insane, or, if so, at what point he became
impaired to the degree that the murder became unstoppable.
And that, of course, is the question that really causes
concern. Did Griffiths, and by implication, people like him,
truly have free will? Or were they merely a bundle of
neuroses and fragments of shattered psyche waiting for the
unfortunate combination of neurotransmitters that would
trigger them like a bomb? Do they choose to do what they
do? And if they do, do they know it to be wrong? And if
they do know, do they care? Are they remorselessly driven to
destroy others, and ultimately themselves, like a virus?
Worse, if a particular set of circumstances had not occurred,
could Griffiths, and his victim, have gone on to live normal,

uneventful, blameless lives? If Regan's taxi had come under the bridge two minutes later, or two minutes earlier, would Griffiths still have flagged it down and commenced his fatal journey? Certainly, an opportunity to learn about what had triggered Griffiths' frenzy in May 1948 was missed, when the medical evidence was denied an airing, and this may have led to a delay in detecting, and possibly preventing, other murders. However, it seems clear from reading the documents available, that Griffiths made a conscious decision to go to the hospital on the fatal night for whatever reason. Probably, he did not have at that time any clear action in mind. We do not know at what point he took it upon himself to take a child, or whether he actually had a predetermined plan as to what he intended to do with them when he did so, or what attracted him so to poor June Anne rather than the others. But he clearly knew at some level when he took his shoes off, when he covertly entered the ward, when he took the heavy bottle to defend himself, that what he was doing was very, very wrong.

And if there is a lasting horror, one that is liable to keep someone awake at night if they contemplated the true ghastliness of his actions, it is the one that Griffiths himself described in his confession. The image of a man, leaning over a cot, lifting out a crying toddler and, as he takes her to her doom, holding her with his left arm and gently supporting her with his right, resting her head on his shoulder to comfort her as he walked her into the dark cool of the night from which she would never return. That, if nothing else, is a clear picture of evil at work. Whatever one's opinion of judicial execution, of capital punishment, whether it is a deterrent or not, whether it is a sign of an unethical society or not, execution was a valid penalty at the time, and for that one single terrifying, burning, terrible portrait of twisted compassion alone, it was well deserved.

Chapter 28

Loose Ends

In his biography, Capstick makes note of a grim postscript to the conviction of Peter Griffiths. Let us not forget, his first trip to Lancashire was to deal with the murder of Quinten Smith. In reality, the murder of poor Quinten was never anywhere near being solved, but this was not for want of trying. It is possible that if the death of June Anne Devaney had not intervened, that the matter would have had Capstick's full and undivided attention, and that he would have eventually uncovered the murderer. It is possible that this killer would have been the same man who attacked girls in the area a few years before. Sadly, we will never know. Capstick turned his fearsome powers on the tracking and arrest of Griffiths, and in his hubris, he decided that the two killers were one and the same. Not such an unreasonable assumption, one supposes. Farnworth and

Blackburn are only half an hour apart by train and road. To Capstick, and to many, it was inconceivable that such a small geographical area could produce two separate child killers who both struck within a month. Logic therefore dictated that the crimes *must* be the work of the same man. Never mind the fact that apart from a blue suit, the descriptions of the killers were quite different. Never mind that the *modus operandi* were opposite ends of the scale, one opportunistic, the other seemingly planned, albeit to some wild, unknowable extent. Desperate to prove his theory, Capstick persuaded David Lee and his parents, and the authorities, to allow David to visit Griffiths in Walton Gaol, to see if he could close both cases.

And so, before he was executed, Griffiths had a visitor. Accompanied by Capstick, David Lee arrived in Liverpool. Although he was interviewed about this event in later life, Lee has never revealed to the public what his feelings were on this day, what excitement or trepidation he felt as he walked down the long, echoing corridors towards the wing where the condemned prisoner was held. Don't forget, this was a child, being taken to face his worst fear. Through the prison gates, down the barred corridors, footsteps echoing as they neared the final cell. They entered a solitary room, to meet Griffiths, the same sallow youth that Capstick remembered, a trifle thinner perhaps. Capstick asked David flat out if he recognised Griffiths as the man who had attacked him and killed his friend. David stared at him for a long moment. What went through his mind at that time, for those few, long seconds when he came again face to face with a monster? But, not *his* monster. Griffiths was not the man. Too tall.

The Cottontown Killer

David Lee was returned home, and eventually the police guard that had been placed upon him for protection was removed. He went on to live a full life, although what horrors may have haunted him, only he knew.

Capstick was more than disappointed, but he was not downcast. In his opinion, Griffiths was the most likely murderer of Smith *and* any other child that had met a bad end in the north west recently. The relevant chapter in his autobiography finishes in this manner:

'...I am convinced that when [Griffiths] died he took with him the secret of the 'mad moon killer' of Farnworth. There were no more child-murders in Lancashire.'

But of course, Capstick was wrong, and this is where the blinding certainty that had served him so well strayed into arrogance. For him it was 'job done', one crime solved the other as good as. But this was of course not the end of child murders in Lancashire, and, sadly, it could never have been so. The human condition is infinitely variable, but there are various recurrent archetypes thrown up again and again by accident of probability, genetics, nature and nurture. After all, human beings are merely sentient machines, programmed by evolution to respond to stimuli in only a handful of ways, behaviour governed by a finite number of protein interactions. Griffiths was a misanthropic, disturbed loner, whose sullen urges had been brought murderously to the surface. Whether it was nature or nurture or both that were responsible, it was unlikely that such an individual would not emerge once more from the shadows.

Inevitably, only a short time would pass before Capstick was to be proven wrong. Six years later, a series of child murders in nearby Wigan once more shook the country. The first death occurred on June 19th 1954, when six-year-old Wilf Schofield was found dead on wasteland in Ince-in-Makerfield, having been stabbed the night before, a Friday. The boy had received five stab wounds in total, the fatal one having penetrated between the ribs to the heart. It soon emerged that Wilf had been last seen playing with two other boys, and they had fashioned a primitive spear by mounting a penknife on a stick. Both these boys were given alibis by their parents. However, eventually they admitted to playing cowboys and Indians with Wilf, using the spear. During the horseplay, the unfortunate Wilf received the fatal injury and the two other boys, scared witless, fled. During the Inquest, a failed attempt was made to retract the confessions. Due to their age, and the accidental nature of the death, neither boy was prosecuted. However, because of the repeated adjournments of the Inquest, the case was not entirely settled until September. Partly, the delay occurred because proceedings were derailed by the death of another child in August, which bore uncanny similarities to that of poor Wilf. On Friday 27th August, a 999 call was received at Wigan Central Station, stating that a boy had been found injured at Miry Lane. A passer-by had responded to a call for help, and found the boy crawling, obviously wounded, on the ground. The boy asked if he was still alive. When asked who had attacked him, he replied simply 'It's a man.' By the time the Police arrived, the boy had been moved to his home in Vere Street, a short distance away. APC Ashurst found him prostrate on a sofa, drenched in blood. The boy, William Harmer, 11 years old, was declared dead a short while later at the Wigan Infirmary. Harmer had been in care, and as a result had received elocution lessons, and was noted around the area for his posh pronunciation. His loss was widely felt. Post mortem examination confirmed that the lad had received ten wounds from a knife. A team from Scotland Yard, led by Detective Chief Superintendent Colin McDougall took over the investigation. It was then discovered that another boy had been attacked earlier in the same evening.

Seven-year-old William Mitchell had been messing about by the canal with his chums when they decided to climb over a wall to play in a nearby yard. William, the last one over, was accosted by a man who asked him what he was doing, and then demanded that he come with him. When William refused, he was seized and attacked with a knife. The man fled when two passers-by responded to the boy's cry for help. Fortunately, William had only suffered a superficial injury. He described his attacker as 5 foot nine inches, 'more of a big lad rather than a man', thin, with blond hair, blue suit, no tie

A widespread search was instituted, centring on men who had recently put suits in for cleaning. Amongst those interviewed were two brothers, Alexander and Norman Green. Norman, a blond with almost white hair, known occasionally as "Snowy", stated that he was at home in bed unwell at the time of the attacks. His mother corroborated this story.

No progress was made on the case until a third attack took place on April 11ᵗʰ 1955, Easter Monday. Ten-year-old Norman Yates was found dying in a back alley from a stab wound in the neck. Norman had been sent out by his mother to borrow some last-minute groceries from his aunt who lived up the road. Police enquiries revealed that a blond man had been seen nearby. The search for this man became the priority, and the police interviewed every blond they could find, publicised the description and the services of professional wig makers were employed to determine the exact shade of hair of the main suspect.

The break in the case came when a PC Hardman remembered that a month previously he had briefly interviewed a blond man answering the description who was acting suspiciously at a fairground. The man gave his name as Norman Green. On 15th April, Green was interviewed at his place of work and asked to give an account of his movements. His story was inconsistent, and in the meantime, officers raided his house and found clothes matching the description given by witnesses. Green told the police he was not the man they were looking for. They wanted someone like Straffen, he said. Straffen had murdered two girls in 1951 and was committed as unfit to plead by reason of insanity to Broadmoor Asylum. He escaped in 1952, and immediately killed again. A second murder trial followed, and he was sentenced to death, but reprieved for insanity. He eventually died in 2007, having never been released. At the time he died, he was Britain's longest serving prisoner. Green repeatedly referred to Straffen avoiding being hanged by cause of insanity. He gave an official statement, denying everything. However, the forensics betrayed him. When faced with the evidence, he suddenly confessed that he got an urge which he could not fight against. He gave a full confession, which he finished with the words 'I am very sorry; and I am very sorry for the mother. I hope she forgives me for what I have done.'

Despite his efforts, Green was judged not to be insane, and was executed on the 27th July 1955. There are many locally who still believe that the unfortunate Wilf Schofield was Green's first victim.

The death of Griffiths clearly did not stop the mournful string of child murders that continue into the modern age. However, although Capstick was wrong on this point, he was able to retire from the scene with the knowledge of a job well done. Griffiths was guilty of the terrible end inflicted on June Ann Devaney, and determination and pragmatism, and firm leadership had won out against almost insurmountable odds in bringing him to justice.

Endings

All that is left now is to round up the histories of the players, main and supporting, whose lives are known or findable.

Despite Capstick's certainty that Griffiths was the killer, Quinten Smith's murder remains unsolved to this day. Had he not been distracted by June Anne's murder, Capstick would no doubt have applied his fearsome personality to the events at Farnworth and would eventually found his man. Despite a freedom of information request, the documents regarding the murder remain classified at the National Archive, sealed for many more years, on the grounds that information contained within may cause distress to those still alive, or their relatives. Perhaps within those notebooks, and records, and statements and fingerprints there are the words of the killer, inadvertently captured. After 80 years, the likelihood that Quinten's murderer will be identified is negligible.

Margaret Allen, the cross-dressing murderer from Rawtenstall was found guilty, and was executed at Strangeways on January 12th 1949: the first woman to be hanged since 1936. A petition for clemency gathered only 162 signatures. Her last request was to die wearing men's clothes. This comfort was denied her. Some regard her as a martyr to gender politics.

Sydney Silverman died in February 1968, in hospital in Hampstead. In his life, he had worn many hats: socialist, establishment MP; conscientious objector, anti-fascist; man of the people, intellectual. The one thing he had always been was true to himself, and his core beliefs. He continued to campaign for the abolition of capital punishment after the execution of Peter Griffiths, even though he must have known that it was his own machinations that had led to the opportunity to restrict its use in 1948 being lost. He did however live long enough to see abolition come to pass. Following the second Royal Commission, which reported in 1953, Silverman sponsored Bill after Bill until at last he piloted the 1965 Murder (Abolition of Death Penalty) Bill through Parliament, which meant that the final executions in Britain occurred in 1964, and that the last 16 death sentences passed were automatically reprieved. The full abolition of the death penalty was reaffirmed in 1969. He also lived long enough to see the public outcry that resulted from the notorious Moors Murderers, the child torturers of Manchester, escaping the noose for a life of incarceration; and in the 1966 General Election, his main opponent was the uncle of their victim Lesley Ann Downey, who stood on a pro-hanging ticket. The abolition of capital punishment was both his legacy, and his curse.

The campaigner Violet van der Elst died largely forgotten in a nursing home in Ticehurst in Sussex in 1966, having expended most of her fortune on the abolitionist cause. Presumably she had the satisfaction of knowing that she had at last succeeded in seeing judicial executions stopped.

John Bennet Stoneman, who had so often been Capstick's right hand man, died prematurely in 1949, in unusual circumstances. Part of the Yard's duties was to repatriate British Nationals who had been arrested abroad back to the UK. In 1949, Stoneman was sent to Austria to escort murderess Margaret Lauchlan Williams back home for trial. Margaret, an attractive blonde, was a WRAC assigned to the RAF in Klagenfurt. A disturbed young woman, who in the end admitted to lesbian tendencies, she had married a much older man, Squadron Sergeant Major Montague Cyril Williams, nicknamed 'Slim', in April that year. She was 'fond' of him, and he was smitten with her, but she married him out of pity and convenience more than anything else. The marriage was unsurprisingly not entirely successful, however, and Margaret took to drinking. Heavily. And according to her own account, the marriage was never consummated.

On 4th July 1949 she and her husband had yet another row, which culminated in her stabbing him to death in their quarters. It seems that the row had gone on all evening in several locations and had involved Margaret assaulting both Monty and two other soldiers who had intervened. On return to their quarters, Margaret claimed Montague lost his temper and beat her, although forensic witnesses found little evidence of an assault on her other than some superficial bruising. She always claimed that she stabbed him during the beating. Margaret was later found running up the corridor, covered in blood. It seems that she immediately regretted killing her husband, whom she described often as a 'fine man'.

The post mortem did not support her version of events, however. It was found that Montague had in fact been stabbed twice, once superficially through his shirt, and once fatally when he was shirtless. Opinion was that he had been first stabbed weakly in the arm and had sat in a chair and taken his shirt off to examine the wound, at which point he was stabbed a second time, with force in the chest.

Stoneman flew to Austria, formally arrested her, and flew her back the UK. Margaret Williams was found guilty and sentenced to death in a sensational trial. Her sentence was later commuted to life imprisonment. However, soon after handing her over to the appropriate authorities, Stoneman suddenly became unwell. Very little is known about what happened, but he was admitted to St Thomas' in London, where, despite treatment, he died. It was rumoured that he had been poisoned, although it is more likely that he developed one of those illnesses that modern medicine could have resolved without breaking into too much of a sweat. Stoneman left an estate valued at £876, a substantial sum at the time.

Cornelius George Looms kept the promise that he had made to the people of Blackburn when Capstick had first proposed his audacious plan for the manhunt. Once Griffiths had been executed, he supervised the destruction of the fingerprint cards, save for a few that individuals wished to keep as morbid souvenirs, or out of personal interest. The event made national news and there are many photographs of Looms smiling broadly as the pulper did its work. As the cards were turned to mulch, so a grim chapter was closed. Looms and Campbell wrote an account of the murder and its investigation which was published privately to act both as a historical document, and as a textbook for the education of future police officers. The slim, green volume contained a first-hand account by Looms of the investigation, and a clear record of the forensic evidence and how it was collected by Campbell. Sadly, the victim's name was misspelled in gold leaf on the cover as Jane-Ann Devaney. Looms, so fastidious and precise, must have been distraught at the error.

Looms deserved a long and relaxed retirement. Instead, he died in harness on the evening of Wednesday 7th May 1958 having served the people of Blackburn well. Looms had suffered from failing health for some time, having been treated for a coronary thrombosis at the Blackburn Royal Infirmary a few weeks previously. He did, however, have hopes of a full recovery and had returned to his duties as soon as possible. On Monday 5th May, he attended a benefit for the Blackburn Rovers Football Club players, who were undergoing something of a renaissance. A picture of the worthies at the ceremony shows him standing at the far right of the second row, smiling broadly in his full-dress uniform, obviously enjoying himself. On the evening of the 7th, he was taken suddenly ill at his home, *The Lawns* on Duke's Brow, near Beardwood Old Hall on the west side of the town. One can imagine the despair of his wife, Mary, as she rang for the doctor or ambulance from their phone, Blackburn 4601. He was taken back to the Royal Infirmary but died soon afterwards. He was sadly missed across the Borough, and it was said that the police force had lost a true friend. He was buried at nearby Pleasington Cemetery, now part of the large Witton Country Park. His funeral was attended by many notables, including the Mayor and many of his Chief Constable colleagues. The town turned out to watch his coffin, topped by his ceremonial sword and his police cap, make its way to his final resting place. He was described in obituaries as a 'big, kindly man'. It was almost ten years to the day from the murder of June Ann Devaney. The public had lost a tireless servant. He was 62 years old.

As far as we know, John Capstick never returned to Lancashire in a professional capacity again. His career did not end there though. He continued to have a successful run as a Scotland Yard Man and was lauded by the press as 'one of the world's great detectives.' His last ever murder case was also the sad killing of a young girl, Edwina Taylor, abducted on his own patch in Norwood by Derrick Edwardson, a known sex offender. Edwardson received a life sentence on 25th October 1957, mainly because the girl's parents were against the death penalty. It was the case that led to the creation of what eventually became the Sex Offender's Register.

Capstick retired from the Metropolitan Police in 1957 and took up a post as Chief Security Officer of Garfield Weston Biscuits. In his time, he had faced down desperate and armed gangs, ruthless killers, blackmailers and rapists; career criminals and pathetic one-off wannabes and losers. He had been a good copper, but his era was coming to an end. Police work was changing, becoming more sophisticated, less dependent on the determination of individuals, more dependent on science and procedure. Capstick became a minor celebrity, writing his memoirs, and giving occasional interviews, playing up his reputation as one of the Yard's Big Beasts. He deserved a long time in pasture, growing his roses, and playing bowls, one of his favourite hobbies. It was not to be. He died in 1968 from a stroke. He had his faults, like all of us. He was self-righteous, opinionated, out of touch; but he was fanatically dedicated to policing, to bringing criminals to book, and, insanely brave, he often went repeatedly on the front-line toe-to-toe

217

with the hardest of desperate men. Despite the battering that his reputation has received in relation to the Curran case in recent years, truly the world was a little safer when he had been walking it.

His legacy is largely forgotten, save for one last footnote: in the 1980's, Leicestershire was terrorised by a serial rapist and murderer of young women. Fortunately, the police had a semen sample that would make finding the killer easier. By a stroke of luck, at the nearby University, pioneering scientist Alec Jeffreys had developed a technique by which samples of DNA could be extracted from bodily fluid and compared. Citing the investigation into June Anne's murder over thirty years previously, the police launched a campaign to take DNA swabs and specimens from local men, all of whom were encouraged to come forward by a publicity campaign which mimicked that initiated by Capstick. Over 5000 samples were taken without success, until someone confessed that they had been persuaded to give a sample in place of a friend. This friend, Colin Pitchfork was the first ever killer detected by DNA profiling. The science had changed, but the policing principle had been Capstick's. The big detective had cast a long shadow.

References

Researching this story after I first heard it took a great deal of time. I am indebted to my friends at Blackburn Central Library for their assistance.

Books and Articles

Abbott G Severed Heads: British Beheadings Through the Ages 2000 Andre Deutsch

Allen C The M'Naghten Rules British Medical Journal 27/11/48

Beattie D Blackburn: A History. 2007 Carnegie Publishing Ltd

Begg P Skinner K The Scotland Yard Files. 150 years of the CID 1842-1992 1992 Headline Book Publishing

Bennett W The Pendle Witches 1993 Lancashire County Books

Blackburn: Past and Present Maps 1844- present day 2007 Cassini

Bland J The Common Hangman. English and Scottish Hangmen before the Abolition of Public Executions 2001 Zardoz Books

Block BP Hostettler J Hanging in the Balance. A History of the Abolition of Capital Punishment in Britain. 1997 Waterside Press

Bondeson J Murder Houses of London 2014 Amberley publishing

Bryson G Shakespeare in Lancashire 1998 Sunward's Publishing

Capstick J (with Thomas J) Given in Evidence 1960 John Long Ltd 1960

Carswell LCJ The Queen vs Iain Hay Gordon : Judgement
http://www.courtsni.gov.uk/en-gb/judicial%20decisions/publishedbyyear/documents/2000/2000%20car%203298/j_j_carc3298.htm Retrieved 20 August 2020

Clarke G Trial of James Camb. Notable British Trials Series 1949 William Hodge & Co Ltd

Eddlestone JJ The Encyclopaedia of Executions 2002 John Blake publications

Egerton Lea Consultancy Ltd Witton Park, Blackburn Historic Environment Desk Based Assessment 2009 http://www.blackburn.gov.uk/lists/downloadabledocuments/witton-park-historical-report.pdf Retrieved 20 August 2020

Fielding S Lancashire Murder Casebook 1994 Countryside Press

Fielding S More Murderous Bolton 2010 Amberley Press

Fortney WS Full Particulars of the Dreadful Murder of Emily Holland 1876 Catnatch Steam Press, London

Granshaw L Porter R The Hospital in History 1990 Routledge

Godwin G The Trial of Peter Griffiths. The Blackburn Baby Murder. Notable British Trials Series 1950 William Hodge and Co Ltd

HC Deb 14 April 1948 vol 449 cc979-1098 New clause (suspension of death penalty) Hansard

HC Deb 15 July 1948 vol 453 cc1411-545 (suspension of death penalty for murder) Hansard

HC Deb 15 February 1972 vol 831 cc246-54 (Whittingham Hospital Inquiry) Hansard

HC Deb 06 July 1983 vol 45 cc384-8 (Queen's Park Hospital, Blackburn) Hansard

Hayhurst A More Lancashire Murders 2011 True Crime History

Hodge JH Famous Trials 3 Penguin 1950

Kirby D Scotland Yard's Ghost Squad. The Secret Weapon against Post War Crime 2011 Pen and Sword

Kirby D The Guv'nors Ten of Scotland Yard's Greatest Detectives 2010 Wharncliffe True Crime

Lee S Classic Murders of the North West 1999 True Crime Library

Mallalieu J The Man Who Can't Be Wrong. The New Statesman 5th May 1956

McLaughlin S Harry Allen: Britain's Last Hangman 2008 True Crime Library

Medico Legal Correspondent National Insurance. The Court of Inquiry into the remuneration of Insurance Practitioners. Supplement to the British Medical Journal 22nd December 1923

Medico Legal Correspondent Schizophrenia and Responsibility British Medical Journal 13 November 1948

Obituries Bulletin of the Royal College of Psychiatrists p223 vol 10 1986 The Journal of Mental Science vol LXIX http://archive.org/stream/britishjournalof69royal#page/n5 /mode/2up Retrieved 20 August 2020

Pakenham Walsh R The M'Naghten Rules British Medical Journal 11/12/48

Palfrey WJH The Wigan Murders The Police Journal p 267 June 1963-286

Parker Roy Hoddleston and its Satellite Villages: Blacksnape, Eccleshill, Yate & Pickup Bank 2012 Scotforth Books

Sewart A Murder in Lancashire 1988 Robert Hale Ltd

Teignmouth Shore W The Trial of Frederick Guy Browne and William Henry Kennedy Notable British Trials Series 1930 William Hodge and Co Ltd

Wensley FP Forty Years at Scotland Yard 1933 Doubleday

Winchester J Remarkable Cases of Circumstantial Evidence. Bradford the Innkeeper. The Evergreen vol 1 p 268 1840 NYC

Newspaper Archives

Blackburn Times 23/11/35 Husband's death sentence quashed. Wife's to stand.

Britton, Paul (15 February 2007). Search continues 60 years on. *Manchester Evening News*. M.E.N Media. https://www.manchestereveningnews.co.uk/news/greater-manchester-news/search-continues-60-years-on-1119203 Retrieved 20 March 2016.

Carter H **Search for girl's body after 57 years** *The Guardian* **Wednesday 6 June 2001**
     https://www.theguardian.com/uk/2001/jun/06/hel encarter Retrieved 20 March 2016

Cowan R Cleared of murder, after 48 years the Guardian 21 December 2000
     https://www.theguardian.com/uk/2000/dec/21/rosieco wan Retrieved 20 March 2016

Daily Herald Boy,16, accused of killing brother 10 July 1948
https://www.britishnewspaperarchive.co.uk/viewer/bl/000 0681/19480710/059/0003 Retrieved 20 August 2020

Metro Diary of a Hangman up for sale 20 October 2008
metro.co.uk/2008/10/20/diary-of-hangman-up-for-sale-55445/ Retrieved 20 August 2020

Manchester Evening News April-November 1948

Northern Telegraph April – November 1935

Northern Telegraph April- November 1948

Online Sources

Britain on Film Without a doubt, the King of Cotton Britain On Film - Lancashire's Time for Adventure (1948) **https://twitter.com/BFI** Retrieved 20 August 2020

British Pathé News Big Robberies Alarm Authorities (1958)
https://www.britishpathe.com/video/big-robberies-alarm-authorities Retrieved 20 August 2020

British Pathé News Should hanging go? (1948)
https://www.britishpathe.com/video/should-hanging-go Retrieved 20 August 2020

Cottontown website How the Blackburn Poor Live. Fed on less than two pence a day. Blackburn Times June 1912 http://www.cottontown.org/Health%20and%20Welfare/Pages/Hospital-and-Health.aspx Retrieved 20 August 2020

Cottontown website The murder of June Anne Devaney http://www.cottontown.org/page.cfm?language=eng&pageID=5144 Retrieved 20 August 2020

Ellis J Blog 1 Whittingham Mental Asylum John Ellis Historyoflancs

James Watts & Thomas Watts

https://johnellisbfc.wordpress.co/2012/07/22/historyoflancs-blog-1-whittingham-mental-asylum-preston Retrieved 20 August 2020

Essex Police Memorial role of Honour
http://www.essex.police.uk/memorial/roll-of-honour.php?rollOfHonourId=35

Historic Bolton Sheila Fox Unsolved Murder of 1944
http://www.historicbolton.yolasite.com/sheila-fox.php

Holt F Farnworth tales
http://www.boltonrevisited.org.uk/s--farnworth-tales.html
http://murderpedia.org/

Lancashire Police Federation History of Policing in Lancashire
http://www.lancashirepolfed.org.uk/about/force.pdf

Manchester Medical Collection
https://archiveshub.jisc.ac.uk/search/archives/3a16a63e-3462-380f-913d-3734652ae866?component=934e5d1c-444a-3631-8303-e8ad340b1515

Wordsworth S New Bury as seen by me
www.boltonrevisited.org.uk/s-n-bury-s-wordsworth.html

The Cottontown Killer

Printed in Great Britain
by Amazon